MANAGING MONEY

EFFECTIVE MANAGEMENT SKILLS

MANAGING MONEY

JOHN SCOTT &
ARTHUR ROCHESTER

Sphere/British Institute of Management

First Published by
Sphere Books Ltd/BIM 1987

Set in 9/10pt Linotron Univers

Printed and bound in Great Britain by
Cox & Wyman Ltd, Reading

Contents

Preliminaries

If you've picked up this book because your living expenses are always outrunning your income, you're going to be disappointed. This is a book about organisations' money, not personal money. But assuming you're in a management job – any sort of management job – you should find the book helpful. Supervisor or the head of Global Enterprises Consolidated, your job depends on the way your organisation uses its money, and that's at least partly down to you.

Many managers think there's an easy way out. They're the ones who rely on 'experts'. After all, as an individual you can expect your bank manager to keep a tally of what's in your account, or your solicitor to tell you what to do if you've got a legal problem. So as a manager, what's wrong with your looking to the accountants to manage the money? They're the finance experts aren't they? It's their job!

If only it were that simple. In practice you can't leave the money management to the accountants because it's not that sort of money. It's the money-value in the equipment and supplies and people and activities you manage – the resources of the organisation that have been put in your charge. You can't expect the accountants to manage them! *You're* the person who manages the money by the controls you operate, by the decisions you take, by the instructions you give, by the problems you tackle (or don't tackle as the case may be). Everything you do as a manager has financial consequences. The accountants can help with information and advice, but they can't do your management job for you.

This book helps you to do that job by giving you an understanding of the money at work in your organisation's operations – the 'Money Machine' that is constantly running in any organisation. It explains Profit-and-Loss Accounts and Balance Sheets as basic working documents, and how to interpret them with the aid of financial ratios. It shows how a budget is built up and how it's operated. It throws light on the arcane mysteries of Current Cost Accounting, Marginal Costing, Discounted Cash Flow and Net Present Value. And it's all done in a style that is simple and easy to read.

Managing Money, important as it is in any kind of organisation, is only part of your management task. It's one of the three management priorities defined in the first book in this series, *What is a Manager?* The other two priorities covered in other books in the series are no less important: *Managing Work* deals with the fundamental question of what the organisation is there to do and how successfully it does it – including the bit of the organisation you are personally responsible for. Its market orientated approach has obvious implications for money management and cost control. *Managing People* is about the asset that, properly managed, makes the biggest contribution of all to economy and productivity. To make the most of the resources you command – and of the money involved – you can't leave these other priorities out of the reckoning.

All of these books, including this one, are more than just reading-matter. Each contains exercises that enable you to try your hand at relating principles to practice. For instance the quiz that follows, which gives you the chance to test what you get out of the book: before you start reading, work through the quiz and make a note of the answers you choose. After you've finished the book, look back over the quiz and see how many of your original choices you'd change. Their number will give you some sort of measure of how much you've gained.

Money-Management Quiz

1 What is the connection between money and value?
   a) They're the same thing. Money is the only sort of value that counts in a business organisation.
   b) You can't measure value simply in money terms. The problem is how much value you get for the money that's spent.
   c) There's no connection. The money costs of anything are hard fact. Its value is a matter of opinion.

2 If you want to know how well a business has prospered, which gives you the best idea?
   a) How much cash it has got in the bank.
   b) How fast its capital has grown.
   c) How much profit it has been making on its sales.

3 How exactly can you measure a business's profit?
   a) Very exactly. Profit is money that accumulates in the bank as a result of the business's operations. You simply have to count it.
   b) You can't do it, but accountants can. Their special expertise is needed to calculate the profit very precisely period by period.
   c) No one can do it exactly. Any profit a business declares depends to some extent on managers' opinions of the value of things, and that's not an exact science.

4 What's the difference between a profit and loss account and a balance sheet?
   a) A profit and loss account shows what's happened to the financial picture at a point in time.
   b) A profit and loss account shows what profit the business has made on its capital. A balance sheet shows how its income and outgoings balance.
   c) There isn't any real difference – they're different forms of the same information.

5 What does your budget tell you as a manager?
   a) The financial implications of an operational plan you're working to.

b) How much money has got to be spent by a certain date.
c) The financial limits within which you've got to plan your operations.

6 In working to a budget, what is the aim?
   a) To find out the reasons why any expenditures are above or below budget, and act on them.
   b) To keep all expenditures exactly to the budgeted figures.
   c) Wherever possible to get expenditures below the budgeted figures.

7 'Good liquidity' means the organisation has plenty of cash to pay its bills. Does this have anything to do with its profitability?
   a) Obviously yes. The better the profits, the better the liquidity.
   b) Yes, but not necessarily a good effect. Too much liquidity can reduce profits.
   c) Actually no. They don't have anything to do with each other.

8 If a business increases its sales, what is likely to happen to its liquidity?
   a) It will have more cash available.
   b) It will have less cash available.
   c) There's no way of telling. Liquidity isn't directly affected by sales.

9 What is usually the best thing for managers to try to do to make their organisations more economic?
   a) Cut costs.
   b) Use resources more productively.
   c) Reduce waste.

10 If inflation runs at a steady 5% a year, how long would it take to halve the value of money?
   a) 14 years.
   b) 17½ years.
   c) 20 years.

Managing Money

1. Management's money

There are two kinds of money.

One is the stuff we all *call* 'money'. It's the coins and banknotes in your pocket, the paper figures that represent the same things in your bank or savings account – figures you can easily convert into 'money for real', or write on a cheque or credit transfer form as an alternative to ready cash. It's a thing we reckon we're 'handling' only when we receive it or count it or spend it. As long as you can add and subtract, there's little problem in 'managing' it.

The other kind isn't so immediately obvious. It's the money *values* in things that aren't actually money in themselves, the money that's embedded in an organisation's 'resources'. It's there in physical objects and materials – commodities in stock, equipment being worked, components being processed, supplies being consumed, space being used. It's in activities – people doing tasks, operating machines, handling paperwork, talking to each other, solving problems, looking busy (or otherwise). It's in output – goods made, products sold, services provided, duties performed.

Of course, most of us do have some idea of how this money-in-things works. If we own a house, we know it has a value that we could turn back into cash – and probably more of it than the price we originally paid for the property. Its value 'appreciates', as we say. We might occasionally remember what we paid for other solid assets we possess – a car, a TV set, a washing machine, a piece of furniture. And we realise that what we could resell them for gets less and less as time goes on – they 'depreciate'. But for the most part we don't 'manage' their value, don't even think of them as money-value. They're simply *things* – objects and property that we own or have the use of.

If you're a manager, this money-in-things is the money you manage. You do so – accidentally or on purpose – in almost every decision you take as a manager. Actually, most of these decisions aren't likely to be directly to do with money. They'll be about the physical objects and the processes and the

1

activities and the people you're managing. But money is always involved somewhere. If you've got money sense, you won't forget it. You'll have developed the habit of making the connection between the things and activities and people you *can* see and the money values you *can't*. Whatever the immediate point of the decision you're taking, you'll try not to lose sight of any financial consequences.

Money is the lifeblood of every organisation and institution in our society. And in every organisation there's a limited amount of it in circulation. There's never enough to do everything you'd like. That's why managers need to know what they're doing when they make decisions about the allocation and use of the resources it provides – the materials and equipment and people they're responsible for. Mismanage those resources, and they're literally wasting money. They weaken their organisation's capacity to do the things it exists to do.

If it's a business, the very existence of the organisation might well be put at risk. It becomes an easier prey to takeover or dismemberment by managerially healthier outfits. In really bad cases it develops galloping anaemia – it eventually becomes insolvent, the organisational equivalent to death.

In public institutions, the link between good management and financial fitness to perform hasn't always been so close (not in the past at any rate). That may be why their difficulties are so severe when cash limits are imposed – a kind of substitute for the economic realities that businesses must respond to. But whether or not such pressures exist, the manager in local government or in an agency or undertaking of the State has a duty no different from that of his opposite number in a business organisation: to pay proper attention to the *economy* of his operation as well as to its physical performance.

This isn't just a question of knowing what things cost – although obviously that's part of it. You have also to know how money behaves in your organisation, the 'rules' by which it operates. You have to realise too that there are a lot of things you can't reduce to money terms at all: your people's sense of purpose for instance, or the skill and energy they put into their work, or how effectively they operate together. You can't see them in the accounts, but they have overwhelming effects on things that do appear there. You need to understand the ways your actions as a manager influence the economy and cost-effectiveness of your patch of the organisation – and of other areas affected by what goes on in your patch.

It's a job every manager has to perform for himself. It can't be handed over to the accountants because they're in no position to do it. On the organisation's field of play they're the score-keepers, not the score-makers. True they can advise the players about the state of play, but they neither make the runs nor take the wickets. The decisions about the batting and the bowling and the disposition of the field that govern the score and the scoring rate, decisions like these have to be based on knowledge of *everything* involved in the play. Only the players – the managers and their people – have that kind of knowledge. But they need to know the principles and rules by which the score will be reckoned too.

So the manager has to be able to work with figures and numbers as well as the accountant does. He needs to be able to quantify things – to add and subtract, multiply and divide, calculate percentages and ratios and so on – though the arithmetic involved is usually fairly simple. But this isn't all. He's also got to be able to judge the value of things that can't be represented by figures, to get a feeling for the way they have to be balanced against the things that can be figured out in quantity and cost terms. In fact, there are three basic kinds of reckoning that he has to marry together in his judgements and decisions if he is to manage the money values he's responsible for. The quality of his decisions depends on how good he is at reckoning:
 – numbers
 – value
 – time

Numbers

The manager needs to be 'numerate' – to have the knack of thinking in figures and to know what's important about them.

The basic law of money is that it adds up. Money is stuff you *count*, whether it's money-for-real or money-in-things. And most of the things in an organisation that are countable can be converted into money figures as long as you've got a cost to start off with. Money is the common denominator for a host of resources that are very different in reality but that all share one common feature – they can be figured. For instance:
 – volumes of materials or supplies
 – units of output
 – areas of accommodation
 – items of equipment
 – numbers of employees
 – the hours they spend doing things
Each of them has a cost – the organisation has had to pay a

specific amount of money for them. Given that fact, you can do things with the figures to discover other financial facts about the resources. You can add their costs together to find their total money-value in the organisation – or in any one section or operation that uses some of them. You can divide a cost up to see what the unit cost is – for instance, calculating the cost per hour of people's time or the cost per item of some pieces of work being processed. You can compare one money-figure with another to find out how they influence each other, or to detect a trend, to discover whether you've got a financial problem to resolve.

The trouble is that it's often difficult for the average thinking person to conceive how the arithmetic used in calculations like these can actually show something real about the objects and events he sees around him. As far as he is concerned, once a piece of equipment or an item of stock has been bought, the money has been spent. The idea that the money-value is still inside the thing, disappearing little by little, is just a piece of book-keeping fiction. And the same goes for a lot of the other figure work necessary for management. Many managers find themselves in this fix. Faced with calculations of depreciation or financial ratios or discounted cash flows, the figures numb their minds. The word 'numb-ers' often seems particularly apt!

Yet the point of numbers is at bottom a very simple one. They are a kind of modelling kit that enables us to mimic or predict something happening in the real world. One apple plus two apples make three apples, and you don't have to have the apples actually there to work it out. Pay a parking meter for two hours' parking but leave your car there for three and you're one hour over the limit, and you don't need to look for the parking ticket to know that. The calculations we perform with the figures are useful to a greater or lesser extent – depending on some very obvious questions: how accurately do the calculations represent the situations or events they're supposed to represent? How useful are they at telling us things about those situations that we wouldn't otherwise realise? How easy and simple are they to do?

There *is* a problem. But it's not usually a problem with the arithmetic. Take for instance the operation of adding figures together. After a child has learnt to recite numbers in sequence, 1, 2, 3, 4, 5 . . . , adding-up is the first thing he learns to do with them. But it's a process with two very different aspects:

(a) the operation of adding – knowing the formal laws that sums obey. One plus one equals two; five plus eight equals thirteen.
(b) its application – understanding in what circumstances you add.

The first aspect is easy. The fun begins with the second. Many children know *how* to add but don't know *when* to add. Does the adult know any better?

Try these ten problems that on the face of it are problems in simple arithmetic:

Problem 1: a wine-merchant sells a bottle of wine for £3.00. What will he charge for a case of 12 bottles of the same wine?

Your answer:

Problem 2: you pay a charlady £6.00 to clean and dust around your house for three hours every Tuesday. One week you ask her to do an extra three hours on the Thursday. How much would you expect to have to pay her that week?

Your answer:

Problem 3: a bank charges interest on loans at a rate of 20% a year. If you borrow £100 for two years, what will be the total interest that's accumulated at the end of that time?

Your answer:

Problem 4: the bank calculates your credit rating for the loan by a points system. It gives you three points if you own your house; adds two points for every £5000-worth of salary you earn; adds another point for every three years you've stayed with the same employer; subtracts one point for every year you are below 25 years old; subtracts three points if you have a criminal record . . . What does the sum mean?

Your answer:

Problem 5: a job evaluation scheme uses a points system to determine pay levels: so many points for the skill your work requires, plus so many for the effort it demands, plus so many for the amount of responsibility you carry, plus so many for the number of subordinates you have, plus so many for the value of equipment you control . . . What does this sum mean? Is it different in any way from the bank's credit rating?

Your answer:

Problem 6: under a food rationing system you are given a book of food coupons. Each week you can surrender two pink coupons for a half-pound of meat, and one green coupon for a quarter-pound of sugar. What do the three coupons represent?

Your answer:

Problem 7: a manager records the monthly output of his department as a percentage up or down from the previous month's output. One month he records a drop of 10%. The next month he records a rise of 10%. Does that restore the output to its original level?

Your answer:

Problem 8: it takes one gardener five hours to rake a lawn clear of leaves. If a team of five gardeners did the job together, how long should they take?

Your answer:

Problem 9: it takes one person a day to prepare a report on a job he's been involved with. If two people who've been involved prepare the report together, how long will they take?

Your answer:

Problem 10: if you add one cup of milk to one of popcorn, how many cups of the mixture will there be?

Your answer:

... plus one for amusement: the world-famous painting called 'The Mona Lisa' is valued at (say) £8 000 000. What might *two* Mona Lisas be valued at?

Some of these types of problems do catch people out. But that's just evidence of the numbing effect that numbers can have on the mind. The point of each one is to look behind the figures to what they represent as actually happening in the real world. Only then can you decide whether simple arithmetic answers the question, or whether it's a different calculation you have to perform. It's a problem needing 'common sense' as much as mathematical ability. Let's see how the problems can be answered:

Problem 1: the wine merchant doesn't sell the case at £36 (£3 a bottle). His price is something less – £34 let's say. The £2 discount represents his reduced costs in selling all twelve bottles in one transaction, compared with the extra time and trouble involved in selling them singly. Such discounting is so common that we're all familiar with the way it bends the simple rules of adding and multiplying.

Problem 2: your charlady would expect at least double – £12 for six hours. Possibly more if you're asking her to disrupt her normal

7

Thursday work. Certainly there's no discounting. You're taking an extra three hours' service from her that she therefore can't sell to any of her other customers. And the same applies to the time of any temporary staff or consultants your organisation hires.

Problem 3: the total accumulated interest will be £44 at the end of two years. What some of us sometimes forget is that interest is almost always *compound*, not simple. You can't calculate it by adding two lots of £20 together to get £40. In the second year, the 20% interest will be on the original £100 (the 'principal' as the accountants call it) *plus* the £20 interest on the first year's borrowing:

	Loan	plus	*Interest*
First year	£100	+	£20
Second year	£120	+	£24 (20% of 120)
			£44 total interest

It's important to realise how powerful a device compounding is – whether you're looking at an interest rate or, say, the effect of inflation. Invest some money at 10% compound interest and leave it there for seven years, and you double your money. Simple interest at 10% (if you were fool enough to invest that way) would make you wait three years longer for the same result.

The same works in reverse for inflation. At 5%, money-value halves in fourteen years. At 7%, it takes only ten years to do the same. And inflation has very damaging and distorting effects for the money-values that managers manage, as we shall see.

There is a useful rule-of-thumb to remember in understanding the effect of compounding – *the rule of 70*. Divide the percentage rate of interest (or inflation) into 70: the result is the number of years that rate takes to double (or halve) the money-values involved:

$$\frac{70}{5} = 14 \qquad \frac{70}{7} = 10$$

Problem 4: the sum the bank calculates as your credit-rating is a *figure of merit* for you as a lending risk: the higher the figure, the lower their risk (or that's the theory, at least). It's a somewhat arbitrary figure – an attempt to quantify something that's really a matter of judgement. It would probably be very hard to justify the rating in individual cases. But across the mass of the bank's customers, it might be useful as a rule-of-thumb guide.

True, each element in such a rating method is an objective fact in itself – the house, the salary etc. The question is how far the elements (both individually and in the particular way the system combines them) relate to what the system is intended to measure. Does it make sense to say that a criminal record is offset by owning a house? In particular circumstances, probably not. But perhaps this isn't what the inventors of the system were after.

Problem 5: the sum of job evaluation points is again a somewhat ad hoc figure. But in this case the purpose is to *compare* one job with another. The system tries to measure *job* differentials as a basis for *pay* differentials.

An extra difficulty here is that many of the factors being rated are themselves rather subjective. For this reason, job evaluation systems usually require a panel of assessors to arrive at the ratings. The hope is that any bias in individual assessors' ratings on this or that factor in a job will be balanced out in the total panel's assessment. But it doesn't alter the fact that the figures are again somewhat arbitrary. Sometimes they seem to depend as much on the way a job is described as what it actually consists of doing.

Problem 6: the food coupons represent your weekly share of the meat and sugar that's available. They're the 'money' of a value-rating system that works alongside the economic one (besides the coupons, you still have to pay for your purchases in the normal way). It's a system that restricts what you can 'buy' with each type of 'coinage' – and how much you can buy at a time. You can't use the pink coupons for butter or the green ones for bread. Nor can you stock-pile by spending a month's worth of coupons all at one go.

Problem 7: this illustrates a common difficulty people have with percentages. The answer is no: a 10% fall followed by a 10% rise doesn't restore the output to its original level. It's still 1% below it. But do you see why this is?

Every percentage starts with a *base* – it's so many hundredths of that base. A 10% fall from a base of 100 reduces the output to 90. A following 10% rise is now from the new base of 90. So it raises the output by one-tenth of *that* figure – to 99, not back to 100.

Incidentally, it's exactly the same principle that explains the accumulated interest figure in problem 3. Interest rates are themselves percentages of course. Starting with a given value of money, the interest shifts the *base value* upwards period by period. This year the interest is 20% of £100; next year it'll be 20% of £120; the year after, 20% of £144 . . .

Percentages are a very common way of reckoning quantity changes in many things that managers are dealing with – money amounts, material quantities, time usages, output rates, sales volumes and so on. So it's pretty important to know how percentages work. Understanding the effect of changes in the *base* is absolutely fundamental.

Problem 8: five gardeners working together might well be able to clear the lawn in forty minutes or so. If they take an hour (one-fifth of the time it takes one gardener to do the job), there's something wrong with their effort or with the way they're organising their work.

Visualise what happens. As the solo gardener clears one patch, the leaves still lying nearby are blown back over it before he can clear them too. In any case he has to walk further than the total distance the five gardeners have to cover between them (work it out!). *And he's not being encouraged by the sense of team-work they enjoy.* If you find it difficult to understand things like these, you've got a problem that can't be helping the economy of your management.

Problem 9: two people working together almost certainly couldn't finish the report in half the time it would take one person. Quite possibly it would take them *longer* than the single person working on his own.

Why the difference from the leaf-raking job? It's a different kind of work, that's why. A report, if it's to be a half-decent job, can't be written in bits and pieces – this bit by this person, that piece by that person. It all has to be pulled together in the mind. And if two minds are collaborating on it they've got to spend time discussing ideas, sharing thoughts, arguing out their differences over the way it's all to be arranged. True, they may come up with a better final result. But it will take more time – possibly a lot more time. Brain-work is always more difficult to coordinate than physical activity. The gardeners can *see* what each other is doing; the report-writers have to talk it through. If their joint effort is to achieve any sort of standard, its coordination is bound to take longer.

It's a general principle of coordination that the more people involved, the bigger the problem. The principle is particularly true of brain-work. With jobs like a research project or creating an intricate system or solving a complex problem, a small team working to a longer deadline will almost always out-perform a bigger group that's being pressured to finish quickly. Given the same chance of success, they'll achieve a higher quality of result – one of *greater value* to their organisation. And they'll produce it more economically – at *less cost* in total man-hours.

Problem 10: you'll finish with just over one cup of the mixture. The cup of popcorn will absorb very nearly the whole of the cup of milk without spilling. 'Add' in a physical sense isn't necessarily the same as 'add' in a mathematical sense. Simple arithmetic doesn't take into account the behaviour of the real materials in the real world.

The problems illustrate the pitfalls of simple arithmetic. If you assume everything in real life operates on the simple rule of one plus one equals two, you're in for some nasty surprises. A sense of numbers doesn't mean that. It has much more to do with understanding what the figures can tell you – and what they can't. If you are mathematically aware, you try to read what they're saying in practical terms so that you can avoid making silly decisions or getting yourself into holes. But if you're like the vast majority of managers, you simply don't do this. It's not that you can't. It's not that you won't. It's just that it doesn't occur to you to do it. You are mathematically oblivious.

Oblivious, not ignorant. You are not a mathematical dunce. In any case, most of the arithmetic involved in management is well within anyone's grasp. You need only to become aware of it. It's not difficult to do.

Mathematical apathy is one of the most fascinating aspects of the world of management. It applies just as much to the world of card games too. The supreme example is Poker. Don't let anyone tell you that Poker is a game of luck – or of bluff, flair, ruthlessness, psychology or whatever. A Poker player may lack them all and still be a winning player, as long as his betting is mathematically sound. Let's see why. This isn't a book about Poker, but the illustration won't do you any harm.

Do you know how Poker is played? If you don't, it's enough for our purpose here to know there are two phases of betting. The first is after the deal; the second is after the players have decided whether to stay in the game or throw in their cards. In the first phase you have to make up your mind whether the five cards dealt to you warrant the stake you'll have to pay to stay in the game. That decision is a key decision, and it's mainly mathematical: you must compare the amount you stand to lose (your stake) against the amount you stand to gain (the pot), and weigh that in turn against your chances of winning.

Suppose the five cards you're dealt include four of the same suit. The chances of making a flush by buying a fifth card in the same suit are nearly 5–1 against (there are nine cards left in that suit among the forty-odd cards you can't see). You decide it is long odds-on that a flush will be good enough to win this particular pot. Before you pay your stake, you want to be sure there is enough money already staked to give you a return of at least 5–1 if you win. Simple isn't it?

Yet the great majority of regular Poker players don't pay much attention to the arithmetic of odds. They believe in 'lucky streaks', or are nuts on psychology and tell you that Cecil always strokes his chin when he's bluffing. But they're quite unaware of what their chances are of finding a third ace to add to the two they hold already (8–1 against, near enough). They just buy three cards and hope for the best. Or worse still they cut their chances another 33% by buying two cards in the hope that Cecil will then believe they started with three of something. Even Cecil doesn't bluff often enough to make up for it.

Arithmetic applies just as much to many management decisions. To know when and how to take them, you simply have to stay awake, mathematically speaking. But most managers are mathematically asleep. Amazingly, even top managers can be caught napping.

Take this story for example: it's about an airline whose planes flew regular trans-Atlantic schedules charging rock-bottom fares. The price of a return ticket had been set at £200. Each plane had 345 seats, which looks like a total potential earning per round trip of £69 000. But of course you *can't* fill every seat every trip. The airline would have been doing very well to fill 90% of them regularly – say an average of 310 seats per trip, earning £62 000.

Now for the other side of the sum. *Direct* costs alone for the round trip were £36 000 (for fuel, crew's pay, landing fees etc). On top of that, each trip had to earn *another* £30 000 to cover the airline's heavy overheads. That makes a total of £66 000 that every trip must bring in – 330 seats to be filled on *every single trip* if the airline was to cover its costs, let alone earn its shareholders any profit. In other words, 95%-plus of the total seats available.

What do the figures tell you about the airline's chance of surviving? You're right – it didn't.

Managers who don't do the figuring make bad decisions about little things too – like a supervisor employed by a small firm in Southern England. Four of his people were working for several months at a site half a mile or so away from the main plant. The firm had arranged a supply of milk to the site for their mid-morning tea-break, one pint each morning. Since most of the milk was wasted, the supervisor decided to cancel the delivery. Instead the men would return to the plant for their morning cuppa.

The daily saving? One pint of milk at 20 pence. The extra time the three now spent walking to and fro each day? Two man-hours at £3 per hour. That's the kind of stupid little waste that's caused time and again by managers who don't think figures. Individually each bit of waste might not amount to much, but put together the bits add up to a sizeable and continuous draining of resources.

It doesn't help an organisation if its managers are blind to the simple basics of numbers. The great advantage of reckoning things in terms of figures is that it forces you to think with more precision than you'd be likely to do otherwise. Suppose you know that your people's time is being wasted in waiting for work, or by the requirements of some ill-conceived system – but you don't know how much time. You may not feel any great pressure to do much about the problem. However, if you know the time losses add up to a total of (say) fifty hours a week, you're more likely to feel pushed to do something about it. If you also know that the time costs the organisation (say) £5.00 an hour, you can start calculating the bill: £250 a week, £1000 or more in a month, over £12 000 a year. The pressure on you to act is that much greater.

It isn't worth trying to keep managers and supervisors in ignorance of how figures add up in their organisations. Yet even middle managers, most of them, are unaware of their company's financial position, have little idea of what a decent return on capital is, don't know how profit is allocated between dividends and reserves, are ignorant of what goes to employees as pay. Perhaps it's the fault of senior executives who hang on to too much day-to-day responsibility. They fail to delegate genuine power to the middle ranks and the responsibility that goes with it. So their managers are inadequately informed. They don't become financially aware because there's no pressure on them to do so in the normal cut-and-thrust of their daily work.

If the point is important for private enterprises whose financial health is put at risk, it's no less important for public bodies. But few of their managers are equipped to understand the cost implications of the way things are done. Indeed, they often seem naïve in their attitudes to the figures they are dealing with. For instance, there was a comment by the Official Receiver in the London bankruptcy court about a bankruptcy which beat all previous records by a spectacular margin. A property business had failed with assets of £10 000 and total liabilities of over £100 000 000. "This bankruptcy", said the Receiver, "has been described as the world's biggest. But really it is a very ordinary bankruptcy with a lot of noughts at the end."

Waste in public spending is rather like that. Its causes are mostly very ordinary: managers' failures to question the actual costs of things, their lack of interest in numbers or in what they mean, their insensitivity to the importance or value of money, their willingness to turn a blind eye for the sake of a quiet life. Much the biggest part of the waste caused by failings like these is made up of small things that go unnoticed day in day out, often for years. But the net result for the public who have to pay the bill is waste with a very great number of noughts at the end.

Value

Value, in the sense of desirability or usefulness, isn't really an accountancy word. Try asking an accountant "I know that's what it cost, but what's its real value to us?" and see what sort of an answer you get. How anyone reckons the value of something depends more on his aims, his viewpoint, his judgement or opinion – even on his personal likes and dislikes – than on any calculation: what I consider valuable you may regard as worthless. If our interests differ, it may be difficult if not impossible to prove who's right.

Accountancy is a language of figures. It reduces all the organisation's varied resources and activities and people to one single common denominator – money. It then computes the numbers without further reference to the real things they represent: purchase costs, payroll expenses, asset book-values (figures, you'll note, not how useful the assets are), depreciation rates, interest payments, revenues, receipts . . . Some of the numbers are themselves based on judgement rather than fact – depreciation rates particularly. If the answer can't be simply calculated from an initial cost or a precedent, the accountant may need the manager's advice. But mostly his figures refer to actual money-movements somewhere back along the line – facts not judgements.

If you're a manager, you've got to take an interest in the value of things. There's the value of whatever your area provides to its 'customers', whoever they are. There's also the value of the assets you manage. Some are physical assets – a piece of equipment, a stock of material, an area of accommodation, a person's time. Others are less tangible – a person's ability or attitude, a system of working, the way your set-up is organised, the general state of morale in it. They're the *in-*

visible assets – or liabilities – of the organisation. They're revealed in the questions you ask, which often don't relate to figures at all:

- "how well is each of our assets contributing to what we're here for?"
- "are we wasting time and effort in activities that don't contribute?"
- "could we achieve more with the resources we've actually got?"
- "are there things we're *not* doing that would be worth putting resources into?"
- "am I doing enough to develop the value of the resources – could I make more of the equipment and property we're using? What would an improvement in my people's abilities and working methods be worth?"

A sheet of figures doesn't answer questions like these, not directly at any rate. It may indicate you've got a problem. But it can't actually tell you what the problem is – the *cause* you've got to tackle if you're going to make the figures come out right. The manager has to work that out for himself. The accountants can't.

Good economy isn't simply about cost-cutting. But that's the way most accountants see it – and a lot of managers too. As a result they tramline their way to popular but quite in-effective solutions. Is cost per unit too high? Then slash the biggest cost-centres or cut budgets across the board. Are sales too low? Then squeeze prices. Are stocks too large? Then reduce them all by the same fixed percentage. Is cash flow nearing the danger-point? Then stretch out payments to suppliers. Are profits too small? Then exhort everyone to tight-en their belts. But if the manager hasn't found out what's actually causing the problem, his simplistic remedies often exacerbate the trouble – or create side-effects that are equally damaging.

The underlying problem might be any one of a hundred different things – or more likely, a combination of them: bad product design, lack of planning, lax quality control, inefficient systems, communication failures, sloppy discipline, poor training, loose and ill-defined responsibilities, inadequate people in key jobs, impracticable decision-making, muddled aims. The manager who thinks that all there is to economy is keeping your costs low won't even spot expensive weaknesses like these, much less do something about them. Low cost isn't what the real manager means by economy. He means GETTING BETTER VALUE FOR THE MONEY THAT'S SPENT – which is vastly more important than cutting expenditure. It's also *different*. Nearly always it means looking afresh at things that aren't obviously connected with money — the organisation's invisible assets and handicaps:

Work routines are among the most important things to look at, particularly the long-established ones — precisely because they aren't the kind of things you're likely to question. Staff far down the line incur great gouts of expenditure, mostly or wholly unnecessary, which nobody notices because the spending of time, effort and resources is part of the humdrum administrative routine. And they're often not the types of waste that are touched by across-the-board cost-cutting either. To the manager who's under pressure to find some significant economies, they seem quite insignificant. "It's not worth up-setting things," he might argue, "to see if anything can be shaved off there."

The total waste caused by organisational tramlining[1] is vast. But it's composed of countless small and long-accepted features of daily life in each organisation. On the surface there's nothing remarkable about them:
- some large engineering workshops under a rigidly operated DIY policy annually repaired a huge number of galvanised buckets at a labour cost of £16 per bucket.
- in a Government department, one establishment contained a large office which kept all electricity, gas and water bills for the establishment. Meticulously recorded and analysed were bills stretching back to the 1930s.
- in a national company, each area was required to submit an absence analysis to headquarters. Long established as a routine, it was a time-consuming monthly chore for area managers to check the figures and prepare explanations in case of enquiries.

In each case, the question wasn't "can it be done more cheaply?" It was "should it be done at all?" The economic answer wasn't to try to prune the cost but to chop it entirely:
- the engineering workshops stopped repairing the buckets when they realised their purchase cost was only £3.
- the office in the government establishment office was closed down. Another office took on a small extra responsibility for simply filing the bills for a few years before they were thrown away, which was all that was needed. A small fortune had been spent preserving ancient bills as though they were priceless manuscripts!

[1] Another book in the series *What is a Manager?* discusses the problem of tramlining and how it can be tackled.

- the national company stopped the routine analyses when it discovered they were being filed unread at its headquarters. This had been happening for the previous three years since the person who collated and checked them had retired without being replaced. There never had been much point in the exercise, costly though it had been in management time.

Surprisingly, not all managers react this way when they discover that a routine long performed on their patch is rather pointless. When challenged with the waste of people's time or of space or of a resource they're responsible for, some will argue "but there's nothing better we can use it for – it would be idle otherwise." Which turns the normal means-and-ends argument on its head. The sensible place to start is with the objectives – the ends – and then to work out the best way to allocate the resources as the means to achieve them. Any resources that can't be usefully employed are reallocated or dispensed with. There is no need to be brutal about this. If the surplus resources are people, much can be done without wholesale redundancies.

But the upsidedown logic of the 'nothing better' manager takes the resources of people, accommodation and equipment as fixed features of the organisational scenery. His concern is to have something, *anything* to use them for. The kinds of human failing which allow these things to persist are weaknesses we all suffer from – laziness, greed, limited competence, a desire for a quiet life, a reluctance to see jobs and promotion prospects diminish. Where they take control, the continuing waste of resources can actually become the purpose.

All this doesn't deny the immense value of *effective* routines. People's work-habits, the procedures they follow, the policies they adhere to – when such things are efficient and appropriate to what the organisation is there to do, they're important elements among the invisible assets. Totally undemanding once they're mastered, nevertheless they give a sense of work well done, a feeling of useful contribution that supports people's morale and enhances job-satisfaction.

The organisation's structure and its systems[1] are another important non-financial asset or if they're poorly designed, a severe liability: how the work is divided between departments

---

[1] Another book in the series, *Managing Work*, discusses these questions in much more depth.

and sections, the way responsibilities are allocated between people, the procedures by which they all get things done. The waste that poor organisation can cause isn't directly visible in the accounts. They don't reveal the uncoordinated activities, muddled responsibilities, communications breakdowns, non-existent controls, inappropriate decisions – all the results of having the wrong kind of organisation for whatever you're supposed to be doing. But just the same the costs are there. They show up in the excessive stocks, low productivity, poor quality output, late deliveries, dissatisfied customers and all the other economic problems that have long been typical of our public institutions and private businesses.

Take the engineering industry for instance. Fifty years ago, some factories making engineering products by batch production embarked on an exercise to measure their production efficiency. The exercise used three yardsticks: product throughput times, the size of stock holdings, and performance against planned completion dates. The first showed that throughput times could be calculated from the time it took a batch of products to pass through one production process on the factory floor. To find out how long the batch would take to go right through the factory, multiply that time by a hundred: if a lathe operation on the batch took six hours, the batch would need 600 hours of total production time from raw materials to finished goods. The second measure, stockholding, showed that for every £1000-worth of goods sold, there was £500 tied up in stock. Over half of that stock would be in the form of work-in-progress on the factory floor (the result of long throughput times); the rest would be split fifty-fifty between bought-in parts and materials, and finished goods. The third measure, performance against deadlines, looked at the orders issued by Production Control to the different processing departments of the factory. Fewer than half were completed by the given deadlines. A similar check of the Purchasing Department's deliveries of components and materials to the factory found an even worse performance. All the factories were reasonably efficient ones for those days, but these results were considered very poor.

In the late 1970s these same measurements were repeated in a number of modern factories. Over forty years of supposed progress lay between this and the previous exercise. The results were almost exactly the same.

The cause is a general tendency to hang on to familiar but inefficient methods. For example, the following are still quite common features of organisation in our factories that go a long way to explain the problems we've just described:

- process division, seen in its most extreme form in the production line of the old-style car factory – different processes arranged in sequence along the 'track' on the factory floor. This system creates unsatisfying and frustrating jobs for the people employed on it, and yet it's very vulnerable to the resulting labour unrest and stoppages. Another form of process division common for batch production is to make each section of the factory specialise in one process – lathes in this section, drilling in that one, grinding over there . . . Each product batch has to visit several different sections. Different batches require different combinations of processes in different sequences. The result is a very complicated pattern of work flow through the factory, almost impossible to plan and control with any efficiency. It's also impossible to delegate to any one shop-floor manager or supervisor the responsibility for getting a batch completed. Everyone has little bits of responsibility for it, which inevitably means it's nobody's responsibility.

- knowhow division is common in the admin and service functions that support the operational departments. It's usually called 'functional organisation'. Managers and their staffs specialise in very narrow fields of operation. They become very expert in them, but there's a penalty in lack of coordination or sense of common purpose. The system creates a fertile environment for empire-building and political gamesmanship, costly items in themselves.

- multi-cycle systems of ordering. The different materials and components needed to make a particular product are ordered in different quantities at different frequencies – monthly, quarterly, six-monthly and so on. The intention is to enable more economic purchasing. The effect is just the opposite. On the one hand it causes excessive stock-holding of material and components awaiting manufacture. On the other hand it causes production delays, and idle men and machines awaiting materials. Besides which there are heavy losses in obsolete stock whenever products are redesigned.

There's better value in other methods of organisation. They're not of themselves an easy route to greater efficiency and economy – they don't automatically improve things. What they do is to remove the barriers that prevent improvement:

- product division rather than process division. Each department or section is structured as far as possible to

19

achieve a complete end-result by itself – a product assembled, a service provided. The aim is to make each unit of the organisation as autonomous as it can reasonably be. A large manufacturing company is organised into factory units that operate largely as separate businesses. A factory is split into production departments that each contain all the equipment and processes needed to make its own range of products or components. A production department is divided into small teams, each of which produces complete products and is provided with all the machines and skills needed to do the entire job. In shops that are organised into mini-factories like this, most day-to-day decisions about how the job should be done can be delegated efficiently to the supervisors and workers in the groups. There are obvious gains in worker morale and management effectiveness. It's perhaps not so surprising that there are also economic gains in higher productivity, more efficient control of materials and parts, fewer rejects, reduced product costs.

– project division rather than knowhow division. The admin and service functions are provided by small multi-disciplinary teams each containing a mixture of different specialists. Given defined programmes or projects to carry out for the operational units they serve, such teams can be far more efficient than large centralised offices specialising in narrow functions.

– single-cycle ordering – the 'Spitfire' method. At the start of the last war, the resources of plant and materials for building aircraft were very limited. Yet production of Spitfires was pushed to incredibly high rates by the efficiency of the methods used. The key was to restrict the production of every component each month to the exact quantity needed for assembly of Spitfires the following month. Using such single-cycle methods to control the flow of materials through the far simpler systems possible in organisations based on product di-vision, managers can reap big rewards in financial efficiency and economy. They can change their pro-duction faster to meet changes in market demands. They can make big savings in product throughput times and vastly improve delivery performance. As a consequence they can massively reduce the money tied up in stocks and work-in-progress. The net result is to make pro-duction far more reliable, far more efficient – and far less costly.

Good organisation doesn't of itself create good management. But the importance of organisational methods in creating the *scope* for managers to manage properly is often underrated. The point is becoming even more important in these days of fast-developing information technology. Computers provide data – masses of it. But if we lack the organisation and systems to convert the data into usable management information and get it to the manager on the spot, initiative and decisiveness are stifled. So management 'make-up-your-mind' time gets longer and longer, more and more expensive. Sluggishness in management information provision and decision-making wastes resources.

The smaller, more self-contained units of product and project division help with this sort of problem too. And because the decision-making is being done by managers in daily contact with the people who carry out the decisions, there's a better environment for leadership to flourish – which is part of our next point.

People's attitudes[1] often seem to be regarded by the hard, calculating, money-centred type of manager as irrelevant to an organisation's finances. Yet he would probably agree that the productivity of the organisation's people is vital to its economy and financial performance. Perhaps he's assuming you can get productivity no matter what your people feel, simply by coercing and controlling them ruthlessly enough. Perhaps he's convinced that most of his employees automatically have anti-work, anti-management attitudes, and it's useless to try to convert them: coercion and control is all that remains. Perhaps his own psychology gets in the way – he *likes* pushing people around. It would be nice to say he's swimming against the tide. Unfortunately it would be untrue. Many managers have taken the harsher employment situation since 1980 as an opportunity to get the boot off the union and shop steward's foot and on to their own, and to start using it with a fine disregard for niceties like human consideration, fair play and good morale.

Yet there are signs of a change in the climate – an acceptance that productivity needs people's willing participation, their *feeling* that it's important. Attitudes do have financial effects. Well-known and profitable companies are putting money and effort into developing their workforces' commitment, and they're not doing it simply to add to the wealth of human happiness. The wealth they're after has an economic flavour too – in better service to the customers,

[1] Another book in the series *Managing People*, develops this theme.

reduced wastage, lower costs, improved output, increased
market share.

A committed workforce is one of the greatest invisible
assets an organisation can have. But what kinds of commitment have to be built? Basically three: commitment to the
organisation, commitment to the job, and commitment to
managers' leadership. Good management works hard at developing all three, and spends time and money on them:

– *commitment to the organisation*. People need to feel they
  belong. That means keeping them informed about what's
  going on, constantly demonstrating to them that the
  organisation respects and values them as individuals,
  giving them ways to share in the organisation's success.
  Some companies now disclose information to their
  workpeople that a few years ago would never have left
  the boardroom – both operational and financial
  information. There are moves towards giving everyone
  equal status, from eliminating executive dining rooms
  and lavatories to bringing everyone, from directors to
  cleaners, into the same pension scheme. Managers are
  discovering the merits of revealing plans at an early stage
  and inviting their workers to discuss them and offer their
  ideas. It may complicate the decision-making, but the
  commitment gained for making the plans work more
  than repays the extra trouble and cost. And there is a
  rapid growth in share option schemes, productivity

schemes, bonus schemes that enable people throughout the company to see in tangible form their rewards from the achievements they have helped to create.

Now and again there's an opportunity to turn a problem to advantage – as in one company where a strike by the members of one union made the main workforce idle. The company continued to pay its idle workers rather than follow the usual course of laying them off. One of them commented: "Perhaps it will pay off in the future, because the unaccustomed sympathetic treatment did more than anything I've seen since I joined to boost morale and ignite a spark of loyalty. For the first time, many people had a feeling of being indebted to the company in place of the usual union-inspired feeling of being chiselled by it."

– *commitment to the job.* Giving people a sense of status and security in the organisation as a whole is a pre-condition for their interest in doing a good job. But it doesn't of itself create job commitment. Each job has to be designed to earn commitment – which means it must give the person doing it the scope to find interest in it, to feel responsible, to take pride in his performance, even to get excited about the job. Quality becomes the responsibility of the worker on the shop floor, not the preserve of the quality control inspector. Wherever possible, people are directly identified with their own output – like the British bicycles that each carry a tag with the photograph of the craftsman who made it, or the French television sets that each bear the signature of the assembly worker who put it together. Workforce teams are trusted with decisions still generally regarded as belonging to managers and supervisors (obviously this depends on whether teams are a feature of the organisational structure, which was our previous point). Given the chance, they are perfectly capable of deciding their own shift arrangements, of allocating tasks and targets among themselves, of pacing their work, of discovering ways to improve productivity and quality. The result of displaying trust in the workforce and respect for their abilities is usually better performance and fewer emergencies.

– *commitment to managers' leadership.* Without this third element of commitment the other two are less likely to develop. Having a boss you don't respect and feel no loyalty towards can hardly enhance your feelings about your job and about the organisation. And as a manager,

23

the respect and loyalty of your people are things you have to earn. You can't demand respect. Nor can you trade on loyalty. If you don't deserve them in the eyes of your subordinates, you won't get them. Management's credibility with their own people is a vital organisational asset. So how is it earned?

For a start, managers – at every level from director to supervisor – have to assert their authority for decision-making. The weak, uncertain manager can hardly be respected by his workforce. Managers have to find out what's actually going on in the factory, in the office, out in the field, and be prepared to demand effort and good discipline. A competent management doesn't allow itself to become deskbound. Nor does it back away from necessary confrontation. Managers and supervisors down the line have the authority to negotiate firmly with union representatives on day-to-day issues. They have clear objectives and priorities in each area and are expected to keep the workforce constantly aware of them. No compromise is accepted on standards of performance in key areas. People accept tough management if they see it, not as management machismo, but as part of a sustained campaign that involves them too in maintaining standards and competing successfully in a tough economic environment.

At the same time, managers have to be leaders, not just bosses. They have constantly to demonstrate their awareness of the importance of people, and of their desire for a contribution of ideas, energy and enthusiasm from their workforce. Management's own commitment is on the line too. In many overgrown, top-heavy organisations, managers have to be willing to slash the hierarchic levels in their own ranks and to prune the numbers of headquarters' staffs – reducing the management overhead, simplifying the organisational structure, giving line managers clearer authority, closing the communication gaps with the operational levels. They have to be ready to inform, to explain, to listen and to respond constructively to their people's ideas. They have to give a high priority to the development of people's competence and confidence in their own abilities – and not just by formal training. That's important, yes. But managers also do it day in day out by informal coaching, by delegation, by giving their people the opportunity to demonstrate their abilities, by involving them in management decisions. Pompous managerial self-importance is a luxury an organisation can ill afford.

There's a snag in all this of course. It costs management time, effort, patience – and therefore money. You have to put the value of intangibles like feelings and interest and attitudes and self-confidence against the cold hard cash. In simple accounting terms it's difficult to justify the spending, particularly when there are other more obvious money problems about. Maybe that's why accountants so often make rather poor managers. They have a problem in making the mental connections between money and non-money items like appropriate systems and organisation, the morale and commitment of the workforce, the quality of people's performance, the wants and needs of the customers. The managers who can make those connections – and stay continually aware of them as ever-present realities of the organisation's economy – are among the most valuable assets an organisation can have.

The quality of management is basic because all the other invisible assets stem from it. But how do you recognise its quality in a particular organisation? First, by sheer professionalism and self-reliance. Competent managers expect to have the power to make their own decisions without constantly looking over their shoulders for signs of superior disapproval. They expect their subordinates to do the same – whatever level they're at.

Weak management shows itself in slow, uncertain and over-cautious decision-making. There's either constant checking on what subordinates are doing or total uninterest. There's overmuch committee debate, excessive reliance on back-up expertise, rigid insistence on formal procedures and communication channels, and a general disregard of good delegation. Decisions are often wrong because they're made at the wrong level. So there are gaps between the decisions and the reality in which they're supposed to be implemented – like the budgeting system in a particular major transport organisation. Budgets were prepared at lofty headquarters level. Most of the spending was done at the grass-roots level where the budgeting process had never penetrated. A consultancy report on the organisation criticised its senior managers for weakness in the skills required to run a big business, and for a cosy consensus approach to problems. So much for professionalism and self-reliance!

With competent management, decisions are based on a

clear sense of practical realities. Rather than waste time on a lot of over-detailed long-term planning, managers keep a close eye on here-and-now issues. They make time to go walkabout down at the operational level to talk to their people, to see what's going on, to find out what the problems actually are. And they can do this without undermining their supervisors' credibility with the workforce. Middle and senior managers should surely have the wit to let themselves be seen as interested but not interfering!

This attention to practical details is focused by managers' sense of direction. To say that over-detailed long-term plans are a waste of time doesn't mean that planning is pointless. The aims and priorities set for an organisation by its top managers are among the best indicators of the quality of their management. Poor quality management generally has poor quality aims. Take the vague, muddled and even contradictory objectives stated by different board members of the transport organisation we mentioned a moment ago:

- "to improve our level of service to the public"
- "to optimise vehicle miles within the financial resources available"
- "to maximise passenger miles"
- "to reduce costs"
- "to provide better value for money"

No sense of clear-cut mission there. Or take the findings of a survey done a few years ago among over eighty companies in fields ranging from insurance to sweet-manufacturing. Their top managers were asked to rate the priority they gave to some ten different aspects of their operations, such as profits over one year and five years, market share, employee rewards, company prestige, innovation and so on. In the less successful companies, managers were far less discriminating about their aims. Generally they claimed that all ten areas were of nearly equal importance. In each of the more successful companies, managers could pinpoint two or three areas as the really important ones for their particular organisation (surprisingly often these included 'employee rewards'). Among successful managements there's a general opinion that to have a large number of objectives is to have no real aim. There's got to be no disagreement about the direction in which the goals lie.

There's another, even more fundamental touchstone of the quality of an organisation's senior management: the quality of the lower-level managers and supervisors they pick – and what if anything is done about those who aren't up to the job. If you want to find out about the quality of the chief executive's management, look at the quality of the supervisors' and foremen's management. That's not entirely fair of course, because the chief executive probably inherited most of his people, and it can take a long time to raise the standards of the mass of managers in a big organisation very noticeably. You can't go around firing everybody. Nor does a bit of communication provide a quick fix.

On the other hand there have been some astounding examples of organisations revitalised after years of dull mediocrity by a change of leadership at the top. It's done by a rethinking of the corporate aims and long-term strategy, by reorganisation to cut out dead wood and to involve everyone in getting things moving, by a big investment in training. It seems that the management talent is often already there. The real problem is to identify it and to place it where it can do most good. It's something that needs more objective methods of talent-spotting than subjective opinions and personal convictions: "Good fellow, James ... did a cracking job as number two to old Boothroyd ... deserves a chance at that management vacancy we've got ..." The managers involved would hardly be human if they weren't flattered by the feeling of 'playing God' in the moves they decide on the organisational chessboard. But a lot of their promotion decisions are bad decisions because they're based on the wrong sort of evidence. The reasoning is often faulty too. The fact that someone is doing a good job as a clerk or engineer or salesman isn't automatic evidence he'll do an equally good job as a supervisor of clerks, engineers or salesmen. Even in the same function, a higher-level role almost certainly demands different abilities, sometimes even different personal qualities, from a lower-level role.

Management selection is too important an activity for any organisation to leave it to such hit-and-miss methods. Many organisations have tried to find an answer to the problem by using various psychological or 'psychometric' tests which measure aspects of people's personalities and temperaments, their aptitudes, IQs and so on. True, tests like these are relatively simple and inexpensive to administer. There's also a certain fascination in lifting corners of the curtain on other people's inner makeup and the secrets of their psyche. The trouble is that what the tests fail to reveal about people's practical abilities is often more relevant than what they do reveal about personality.

Another approach, called the 'Assessment Centre', has proved itself over the years as a more reliable method. In fact the first regular use of this type of approach was by the army for officer selection – what was known as the 'War Office

Selection Board' or 'WOSB' – during and following World War II. Rather than tests, the method uses personal assessments, but assessments made by not one but a number of trained observers of each of a number of candidates for a management job. The candidates as a group perform various exercises that simulate those done in the type of job they are being considered for. The exercises aren't tests – the interest isn't in whether a candidate 'passed' or 'failed' them, but in the way he tackled each one. The observers aren't outside consultants but line managers in their own organisation, trained to separate objective observation from subjective judgement.

The exercises are designed (usually by professional consultants) to parallel closely the demands of the real-life job. Each observer has the opportunity during the Assessment Centre to observe each of the candidates. He is then required to report to the assessment meeting the simple facts of what he has seen of each candidate's performance and behaviour. The observers individually complete their assessment of the candidate's ability, and only then do they compare their assessments and explain their reasoning.

Compared with psychometric testing, the Assessment Centre method is rather more costly – not least in managers' time (the line managers acting as observers and assessors). But it has been demonstrated to be at least *twice* as accurate at predicting the performance of people in a higher-level job. For any organisation, the quality of its management is too valuable an invisible asset to try to achieve it on the cheap.

We've taken just four examples of the kinds of invisible asset that tend to get ignored in a narrow financial view of an organization: its routines and working habits, its organisational structure and systems, its people's attitudes and commitment, and the quality of its management. None of them are things you can easily put a money valuation on. You certainly can't do it by pointing to the bill for wages and salaries. Manager, staff member or shop floor worker – the poor performer frequently gets paid as much as the good performer. Nor can you see the financial effects in the year-on-year accounts, because so many other things can affect the money results. That a firm is doing well or badly may have little to do with its people's commitment or the quality of its management, but a great deal to do with market or economic forces. Never mind how badly it's managed, a bank does well when the Government insists on a high bank-rate; never mind how committed its workforce, a textile firm goes to the wall if its markets vanish.

But the financial connection is there all the same. Having

the wrong works manager or chief accountant can be just as fatal to an already dicky outfit as paying too much for the warehousing. And an organisation that can't hold on to a fair proportion of the able younger men and women who'll be the main architects of its success and good economy in the medium to long term is throwing money away just as surely as if it regularly dumped valuable equipment from its factory. To understand an organisation's money management and money problems, you've usually got to look beyond the accounts – to the way its *work* and its *people* are managed. You've also got to grasp the fundamental importance of *time* in all money questions.

Time

Time is money as the saying goes, so you'd expect the accountants to take a keen interest in it. The classic definition of economics is 'the allocation of scarce resources', and time is the ultimate scarce resource – absolutely fixed in quantity, irrecoverable once it's gone, and when you really need it there's never enough. The most fundamental decisions that anyone can make are about the use of their time. Yet the accountants' interest in the time–money connection is very patchy.

Time is the basic way of calculating *PRODUCTIVITY*, which is the amount of useful work done by an organisation's people

and it's physical resources in a given time. The important word there is 'useful'. There's a mistaken notion that productivity is all about making people work harder. In some cases perhaps that's necessary, but it's the exception rather than the rule. The real point is to equip, organise and motivate them to work more *effectively* – meaning making better use of the time of both people and equipment.

In fact there's a close link between the productivity of labour and the productivity of 'capital' (the accountant's name for the money invested in plant, equipment, property and so on). The productivity of a transport fleet, for instance, depends on the performance of both lorries and drivers. For the drivers it's measured by the tonnages and distances moved per man-day; for the lorries it's the same measure per vehicle-day. As long as the proportion of lorries to drivers is constant, efforts to improve productivity must affect both equally – whether it's by improved scheduling, double shifting, better routing, faster turnround at loading and discharge or whatever.

As far as management is concerned, improvements like these are part of the *tactics* of productivity (as opposed to productivity *strategies* that alter the number of people involved or the range and complexity of the equipment). Typically they ought to be decisions taken at middle- and lower-management levels – by managers and supervisors who are familiar with the work and the people doing it. The danger is that these levels get squeezed out, whether through unions' desire to talk to the boss or through senior management's desire to have control of everything. Often it's a failure to delegate. As a result we have decision-makers who are out of touch with the details, inexpert and often impractical solutions, bottlenecks in the decision-making process and – worst of all – demoralised and uncommitted managers at those middle to lower levels. Day-to-day productivity tactics simply can't be delegated upwards without causing a mess.

Poor productivity is a general problem in British organisations, both business and public administration. Where managers do take an interest in time, it's typical for them to concentrate on meeting deadlines, and to fail to notice *how long things take to do*. Time and again, comparisons with the performance of other countries shows that the average unit of British output – cars or medical care, banking or local authority services – requires too many man-hours. So at one and the same time we get low pay rates *and* expensive goods and services, particularly when the poor quality of many of them is taken into account.

But the reason isn't usually lack of effort by the workforce. It's more commonly organisational liabilities of the kind we've been looking at: time-wasting routines and bureaucracy, inefficient and top-heavy organisation, poor commitment on the part of both worker and manager, loose controls, lack of real leadership, management's ignorance of what goes on at the sharp end, hazy and muddled objectives . . . all handicaps that lie outside the picture of organisational assets and liabilities painted in the accounts.

Good productivity (which is another name for good time-management) requires managers to pay just as close attention to the value questions we've been discussing as they do to financial yardsticks of performance. Study after study has shown that financial investments in equipment and other physical resources account for only a small part of the total improvements in productivity that are made. The rest come from intangibles like increasing the commitment and ability of the labour force, reorganisation to meet changed market conditions or to make the most of new technology, raising the quality of management.

But if accountant's can't tell you how to improve productivity, they have an important role in measuring it. Time itself is a very precise measuring rod, and it can be used to measure physical work very accurately. Where the accountants can help is in working out the *COST OF TIME*, though the money measure isn't always so precise. Say you're the supervisor of a number of employees operating machines to make a product. You should know how long they take per item; you should also know how much their employment costs for how many hours per week. So it's fairly easy to convert the labour they've put into the product into a time-cost. Working out the time-cost of the machines is a bit more difficult. You might know exactly how much machine time went into making the product and how much the machines cost originally. But you've then got to estimate their total life-span to calculate a cost per hour, and that isn't an exact science. All the same, it's possible for the accountants to work out some sort of figure for it.

What complicates the costing is that *money itself has a time-cost*. It's measured by the *INTEREST RATE* on it. It's a familiar enough idea for personal investments like savings accounts and bank deposit accounts and unit trusts where you receive the interest – or for borrowings like overdrafts and house mortgages and hire purchase where you pay the interest. If the rate is 15% and you borrow £100 for a year, you know you'll have to repay £115 at the end of that time. It's one

31

of the basic laws of money that the cost of the stuff is created simply by the passage of time.

What we sometimes forget is that this money cost holds good for any sort of investment at all. This includes the money an organisation invests in its buildings and land, in the equipment and machinery it buys, in the stocks of materials and supplies it keeps, in the unsold goods its people have made, in the credit its customers are taking. That product your employees made – it cost £100-worth of their time and it's unsold for a year, say. If the money costs the business 15% a year, it's the same calculation as your borrowing. By the time the thing is sold, the labour in it has cost the business £115, not £100.

Your organisation doesn't have to be a business for the money invested in your time and the time of the materials, equipment and accommodation you're using to cost money. The same is true if you work for a local authority or government department. **All** money has a time-cost.

Actually, working out the proper interest rate to apply is a fairly complicated business, because any organisation gets its money from a variety of sources. The basic measure is the current bank rate. That provides a standard to compare all the other rates against. But the cost of the money from the different sources will vary – some may be below, most are probably above that rate. This is only partly because of the different interest rates on the money from different sources; partly it's due to the effects of taxation, taxation relief and investment grants. Bank overdrafts, fixed interest loans, variable interest loans, shareholders' capital, the company's own retained profits – there are different time-costs involved in each one. (Surprisingly perhaps, one of the most expensive forms of money is shareholders' capital.)

The accountant's expertise is really needed in this area, to calculate a standard percentage rate that covers them all. That's the average time-cost of the money used to finance all the company's operations. Generally an organisation will want a return on any particular operation or project at least equivalent to that rate.

But there's an extra complication: *INFLATION*. Through time, money loses value, or you have to pay more for the same thing – from a practical viewpoint there's no difference. The rate of loss is sometimes faster, sometimes slower, but it's always there. It nibbles away at the purchasing power of the money you've got in your bank account – or in the sock under the mattress or wherever. It does the same to the money invested in companies and corporations and state institutions.

A money figure doesn't mean much unless it's got a date against it. On different dates, different figures of money have the same purchasing power. The differences can be small over a short period but in time they get uncomfortably big:

$$£1.00^{1985} = 95p^{1984} = 31p^{1974}$$

Think what this does to the return you get next year from the investment you're making now. You put in £100 and you want to get a return of 15% in *today's* money-value? With inflation running at 5% over the next year, you'll need to get back nearly £121 in next year's money-value:

now		next year
£115	=	£121

Then think what this means for an organisation's earnings and for the money invested in it. At that level of inflation, if its money isn't increasing by at least 5% a year, the organisation is shrinking in real-money terms. Suppose it's got a capital of a million pounds and the inflation rate is a steady 5% a year, and let's say we're starting some years on in 1990. This is how the million has to grow to keep pace with inflation:

$$£1\,000\,000^{1990}$$
$$= £1\,050\,000^{1991}$$
$$= £1\,102\,500^{1993}$$
$$= £1\,157\,625^{1994}$$

At a 5% inflation rate, the different figures all represent the same real money-value.

Of course, the inflation rate *isn't* steady. It fluctuates up and down. In the early 1970s it climbed to a horrific 25% or so a year. Since 1980 it's been reduced to a level of around 4% to 6% a year. But you can't assume a steady percentage rate for it. Equating the purchasing power of money at different times requires a technique called '*indexing*' that we'll explain later.

Remember, these changes in the money figure to get an equal value only compensate for inflation. To get a growth of a given percentage in real terms, you've got to calculate that percentage increase on top of the inflation increase. Suppose this organisation with its capital of a million pounds wants to grow at a real 10% a year. This is how the figures would have to run (still assuming a steady 5% inflation):

capital in 1990:	$£1\,000\,000^{1990}$
plus 10% in 1991:	$£1\,155\,000^{1991}$ (= $£1\,100\,000^{1990}$)
plus 10% in 1992:	$£1\,334\,025^{1992}$ (= $£1\,210\,000^{1990}$)
plus 10% in 1993:	$£1\,540\,799^{1993}$ (= $£1\,331\,000^{1990}$)

In fact you *don't* have to recalculate the interest rates quoted for bank loans, mortgage borrowings and so on. The rates are usually set to allow for inflation anyway. The effect is actually to reduce the *real* interest rates below those quoted. If you borrow £100 for a year at 15% but inflation is running at 5%, the loan is costing you a lot less than 15% because you'll be paying it in devalued money. It's actually something below 10% (to get a rough idea, simply deduct the inflation rate from the interest rate):

next year   now
£115   =   £109.53

All these kinds of time—money calculations should be meat and drink to the accountants. So they're the people who should keep reminding managers of the growth in profit the organisation needs simply to stand still. Year by year it takes more and more money to keep the organisation's capital at the same real value and to pay the shareholders the same real value in their dividends. In fact, far too often the accountants duck the question of inflation and continue doing their arithmetic as though money is the only hard unchanging fact in our organisations. Don't believe it. Money isn't any harder a fact than the attitudes and skill of your work force, or the ability and vision of your management.

What *is* hard fact is *CASH*. That's the 'money-for-real' we started with – the money in the form of coins and banknotes, or the paper figures in cash accounts that can easily and immediately be converted into money-for-real, or transferred by writing them on cheques or credit transfer forms . . . Depreciation rates and profitability and many other aspects of money management are flexible concepts, but if there's anything you can't muck about with, it's cash. And cash always has a time connection. It's the point spelt out in pre-decimal form in the words of Mr Micawber, that memorable creation of the writer Charles Dickens:

"Annual income twenty pounds, annual expenditure
nineteen nineteen six, result happiness. Annual income
twenty pounds, annual expenditure twenty pounds ought
and six, result misery."

Cash appears at various points in any organisation's operations: when it pays its people, its suppliers, its insurers, its lenders and shareholders, the taxman . . . Also when it receives cash from whoever are its sources of funds. The hardest facts about money are the cash figures and the dates they're paid into or out of the organisation. All the rest are financial art-forms.

The first law of money is that if the cash isn't there, it can't be paid out. You owe £50 that must be paid this Friday. You're owed £100 that won't reach you until next Tuesday week. Your own payment can't be made on time. You're skint. Organisations can suffer in exactly the same way. It's called insolvency but it means the same – they're skint. And it's no help to plead that the revenue they're waiting for is much more than the outgoing that's got to be paid. If the dates don't coincide, the embarrassment is just as big. This timing of cash in and cash out is called *CASH FLOW* and we'll have a lot more to say about it later. It's the kind of time-money thinking that brings accountant and manager closest together.

What usually pushes them farthest apart on the time-money connection is the *direction of time* in which they face – towards past or towards future? Accountants typically look towards the past: they're happiest in the role of financial historian. Managers have to look forward: like it or not, they've got the role of financial decision-maker.

Even when the decisions don't seem to be much concerned with money, there's almost always a money implication somewhere. But some management decisions have obvious cash effects – decisions about how much credit to allow customers, about investments to create future earnings or savings, about increasing or reducing the number of people employed. They are the kinds of decision where the manager most needs the accountant's help to interpret the likely financial consequences.

Take for instance a business investing in a new facility –

whether it's a hotel that's planning improvements in its restaurant, or a factory that's setting up a department to make a new product. You might have heard the names of the different techniques that can be used to relate the value of future income (or saving) to present spending. Some of them allow for the effects of interest rates and inflation, techniques such as Discounted Cash Flow and Net Present Value that we'll explain later. The main point of your understanding them is to make sense of an investment appraisal that uses one of them, not so that you can do the thing yourself. That's what the organisation employs accountants for, among other things.

Often these clever techniques get too much attention. Guessing the future is much more a matter of judgement than arithmetic. The management job in planning any new investment is far bigger than the accountancy calculations. A discounted cash flow analysis may be very carefully done by the accountants, but be totally useless because one of its basic assumptions about the future is wrong. The management job is to make those future assumptions as realistic as possible. Suppose you're planning a new product line for instance:

- will it actually sell? What are the trends in the market and in the competition? What could happen that could sink your hopes? How likely is it to happen?
- at your intended selling price, what is the demand likely to be? What might be the effect of shifting the price up or down? Would it make it more profitable or less?
- how big a demand should you aim to satisfy? What capacity should you build into the new operation?
- what will the operation cost to set up? How should its development be phased – a stage-by-stage growth or an all-at-once exercise? What are the likely timings of the cash outflows?
- how are sales likely to develop? What are the likely timings of cash inflows over the months and years into the future?
- what will the operation cost to run? Which costs will vary with the amount of business? Which will stay at a set level? What are the likely timings of these cash outflows?
- what will be the financial effects of delays in the setting-up? Of problems or stoppages in the running?
- how long a life will the operation have before it becomes obsolete or you have to refurbish it? Will there be any further money value in the old plant or equipment that you dispose of at the end of that time?
- what haven't you thought of that could upset the financial applecart?

. . . all cash-related questions that *managers* have to try to answer whenever they're peering into the future of a development. The accountant can give little help with any of them. Ninety per cent of the planning job for an investment is managerial judgement, not accountancy expertise.

The timing of an investment often depends on the way managers forecast a market trend. A common fault in their estimates is the 'straight-line assumption'. Even when they use sophisticated discounted cash flow and other investment calculations, they project future market growth as an un-sophisticated straight line, as in the illustration.

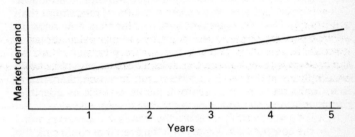

Real life awkwardly refuses to conform. The market demand swings in fairly regular cycles from peak to trough and back again. In a seasonal market (and most markets do have their regular ups and downs through each year), managements know all about this and make allowances for it, even in simple off-the-cuff plans. What they miss are the slower cycles of the economy that operate over years, not months. As a result they often invest at the wrong time.

Boom and recession tend to work on a cycle of about four or five years from trough to trough. (Troughs are easier to see in the economic graphs because they're shorter and steeper. Peaks are less well defined because economic activity tends to run at capacity for longer periods.) So the real pattern of market demand might be more accurately forecast something similar to the following illustration.

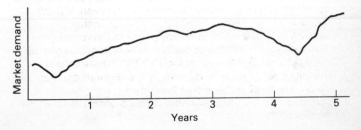

Companies tend to struggle on with the capacity they have until it is fully stretched by a peak in the demand. If they have the funds available, they then invest heavily. Planning, ordering and installing the new plant takes anything from a few months to several years, but averages between one and two years. So the next down-turn is under way before a lot of the new plant is ready. The firm has to wait until the next boom begins, possibly a year or two later, before getting the level of return originally forecast. But by now the accumulated interest on the money invested has increased the return needed to make the intended profit. Besides, the investment is earning that return in money further devalued by the extra period of inflation.

Earlier investment would be better money-management — perhaps six months to a year before a peak in market demand. By the same token, the low point for investment should be perhaps a year to six months before the next trough in the economy. This would not only be more profitable. It would also enable firms to make the most of boom trading conditions rather than be hampered by capacity constrictions and so missing the boat, economically speaking.

Let's try to summarise. Management's money is a currency that comes in many different guises. Often it can't be counted in pounds and pence. It's there in the work performed, its usefulness, the quality of its performance. It's in people, the routines they follow, the abilities they possess, the attitudes they have — pro, anti or couldn't-care-less. It's in time, how productively it's used, how much is produced in a given amount of it, the length of time goods and materials sit waiting to be used or sold, performance against deadlines and delivery promises. There's hardly anything that goes on in an organisation that doesn't have an effect somehow on the stuff you can count.

Assets and liabilities are words we're shortly going to be using in their special accounting sense. But they have a wider meaning too. Managers' own money-sense is never listed among the corporate assets in an organisation's balance sheet — or their lack of it among the liabilities. Yet it has a far bigger effect on the organisation's financial fortunes than physical assets actually valued there in hundreds of thousands, even millions of pounds.

Opposite is a patterned diagram which summarises the first chapter. Each of the following chapters will finish in the same way. This is a feature of all books in the Effective Management Skills series.

The aim is to help fix the main points of the chapter in the mind. We remember things more easily if we can somehow visualise them.

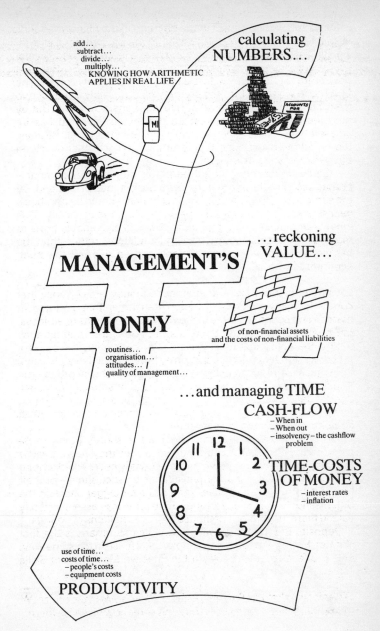

calculating
NUMBERS…

add…
subtract…
divide…
multiply…
KNOWING HOW ARITHMETIC
APPLIES IN REAL LIFE

MANAGEMENT'S

MONEY

…reckoning
VALUE…

of non-financial assets
and the costs of non-financial liabilities

routines…
organisation…
attitudes…
quality of management…

…and managing TIME

CASH-FLOW
– When in
– When out
– insolvency – the cashflow
  problem

TIME-COSTS
OF MONEY
– interest rates
– inflation

use of time…
costs of time…
– people's costs
– equipment costs

PRODUCTIVITY

2. The money machine

Money doesn't just sit in an organisation. It moves around. In fact an organisation is just about the only place you can put your money where it does move. Put it into property or Krugerrands and you don't *want* it to move – that is, you don't want the property to catch fire or the Krugerrands to be stolen, which are two of the ways the money could move. Put it on a horse and you want the money to stay put until the race is run. The horse moves, you hope! The money stands still until you either collect your winnings or tear up the betting slip.

In an organisation, money is *made* to move by the physical operations of the people and things in it – the work it's there to do. When you manage the work, willy-nilly you're managing the money movements too. If you don't understand these financial effects, it won't stop you from getting things done – but it might well stop you from getting them done in a financially efficient way. You're like someone who knows how to drive but doesn't have the first idea of how a petrol-engine works. He gets from place to place right enough, but he uses a lot more petrol than he needs to. The same with money. If you don't know how it works in your organisation, you can waste it without realising you're doing so.

The money machine explains how the money-in-things functions. It's the operation of money that goes on inside any firm, company, corporation or public body. It's really quite a simple operation compared with what goes on in a computer or a television set, say. True, in a big organisation its parts can have very complicated effects on each other, but basically it's rather easier to grasp than the workings of that petrol-engine. In fact, one of the main problems is the jargon the accountants use when they talk about it. The money machine takes the mystery out of the jargon.

We're going to describe the business version – as opposed to that rather different model, the public institution. A business's operations turn cash into products (goods or services) that turn back into cash that turns into yet more products that turn back into . . . In every commercial organisation the cycle goes round and round. At each turn it produces profit – the motor mechanism of the business money machine.

Naming the parts

Suppose you set up a money machine. Let's say it's a company that's going to manufacture and sell pots – moneypots of course. You call it Moneypots Manufacturing Limited.

You need money to start off – to buy the equipment you need, to hire the employees, to purchase raw materials. You also need money to keep it operating. The money doesn't grow on trees. Someone has to provide it.

Question one: where's the money coming *from*?

You've got two possible sources – owners and lenders.

- **Owners**. That's you and anyone else who joins you in the enterprise – your Cousin Fred let's say, who knows next to nothing about moneypots but believes your forecasts of the wealth and riches the business will create. You could be a partnership, but your money machine is a limited liability company so you're both shareholders. Together you put up the *SHARE CAPITAL*. Each of you takes a proportion of the total shares in the company (the 'equity' as it's called) that corresponds to the amount of money you put in – or the money-equivalent (perhaps you'll commit your time and expertise unpaid for a while, or Cousin Fred will provide somewhere to operate the business).

    Naturally you've both got a reason for doing this: *you want your money to grow*. Cousin Fred expects his shares to increase in value as time goes on (so do you, but stick with him for the moment). He also hopes to get a dividend at regular intervals. To get these things he's prepared to take a risk with his money. Perhaps the business will be a great success and he'll be rich. Perhaps he'll discover he'd have done better to leave his money in the bank earning a nice safe 8 per cent. It's a gamble what profit he'll make, if any, and what'll happen to his capital. He can't know ahead of time.

    Nor can you. But the whole thing was your idea in the first place. Cousin Fred is taking a gamble on *you*. He's just a shareholder. You've got two hats – the 'shareholder' hat you share with Cousin Fred and the 'management' hat as the one who's actually running the business. It's an important distinction:
    - as the owners, you're both interested in the growth of the money. That's the purpose of the company for the shareholders.

— as the manager, you personally have also got to be interested in what the company is there to *do* – making and selling moneypots to your customers. As far as management is concerned, profit and money growth are the *conditions* of keeping the company going, not the purpose. The business purpose is to do a cracking good job in the market place. That's the ball to keep your eye on.

— **Lenders**. Your business needs more money than you and Cousin Fred are willing or able to put up. You've got to find another source of money, but you don't want further shareholders who'll dilute the profits and growth you hope to get in years to come. You're looking for someone who'll provide *LOAN CAPITAL* – Aunt Mabel, let's say, who in a manner of speaking *is* a moneypot herself. She'll give you a reasonably long-term loan, certainly more than a year and perhaps as long as four or five years. The loan is called a **long-term liability**.

As a lender, Aunt Mabel has a different reason from you and Cousin Fred for putting her money in. She looks for *interest* on the capital she's lent (which is called the '*principal*'). Apart from that, she doesn't expect any growth in the capital. She'll get a fixed percentage each year, and there'll probably be a fixed period when you have to repay her the principal (whether you pay it as a lump sum or in instalments). All this is spelt out in the contract the company enters into with her, a type of agreement that is often called a 'debenture'.

Aunt Mabel is taking a smaller risk than you or Cousin Fred are. What she gets doesn't depend on future profits. Her interest is deducted before you calculate the profit, and she knows ahead of time what she should get and when. But she still has to be interested in the safety of her money: what **security** can you offer her? That's likely to be a key factor in her decision whether to lend, and what percentage interest she'll want.

Once the money machine is running, the range of lenders widens and you acquire yet another different source of funds. The other source is retained profit, and the new lenders provide short-term money:

— **Short-term lenders**. People and organisations whose lendings happen relatively briefly in the course of doing business with your company: a supplier of goods or services whom you haven't yet paid; an overdraft from the bank; the taxman during the time between a tax liability being created and the tax actually being collected. Individually each lending is a short and perhaps small-scale affair. But taken together the continuous flow of small lendings can add up to quite an important source of funding.

These fundings are accepted as a normal part of business. A supplier, for instance, doesn't usually expect interest on the credit he gives you (though some might give you a rebate for quick payment of a bill – which amounts to the same thing). Normally the benefit he hopes to get is the continuance of your custom, provided of course that you keep to your side of the bargain and pay by the due dates. All these short-term owings are called **current liabilities**.

– **Retained profit**. Your business has a successful year and makes a profit. The taxman takes his slice. You pay some of what's left to Cousin Fred and yourself as dividends. And the rest you leave in the business. It's yet another source of money and one that doesn't depend on finding further investors or lenders.

The accountant's name for this kind of money is **reserves**, which is a misleading term for the rest of us. It makes it sound like a hoard of cash stashed away somewhere against a rainy day – the business version of the sock of money under the mattress. It's nothing of the kind. The money is actually being used inside the money machine along with the rest of the stuff from owners and lenders. Reserves are a *source* of money, not a place where it's kept.

So that answers question one – whose money is in the money machine, and the technical names for the money from the different sources.

Question two: what's the money *in*?

Depending on the sort of organisation you've got and the way you want to run it, there are a wide variety of places where the money could be. Take a sample list of things that most organisations have to own or buy to operate their business,

- land and buildings
- plant and machinery
- vehicles
- office equipment
- furniture and furnishings

- materials and parts used in production
- sales stock
- labour and skills
- leased or rented property and equipment
- lighting and heating
- telephone and postage
- services like advertising, auditing, cleaning etc

But why the dividing line in the middle of the list? Can you see the difference between the items above the line and the items below? It's quite an important distinction for the working of the money machine. Before you read on, see if you can work it out.

- **Fixed assets:** These are the things in the top half of the list, if the organisation owns them rather than renting or leasing them. The organisation buys them to *have the continued use of them* in carrying on its business. The money is locked up in them, so to speak. That part of the money machine isn't on the move.

  What defines whether anything is a fixed asset or not is the reason the organisation bought it. If you buy a lorry as part of your delivery fleet, it's a fixed asset. But if you deal in goods vehicles, it's part of your stock-in-trade, not a fixed asset. You bought it to resell – its life in your money machine is intended to be a short one. Fixed assets, on the other hand, have a longer but nevertheless limited life.

  Spending money on fixed assets is referred to by the accountants as *Capital Expenditure.*

- **Working capital:** This is money spent on things that *get used up* in the organisation's operations, like those in the bottom half of the list.

  Eventually in one way or another they're all converted into stock-in-trade, goods or services that are sold. Some are physical things – materials, commodities, components, parts, sales stock, the vehicle dealer's lorry purchase . . . A lot are things that aren't tangible – the time of employees that is bought with the wage and salary payments, the use of rented property, the flow of orders promoted by advertising and selling expenditures, the information exchanges bought with telephone and postal charges, the goodwill produced by the credit allowed to customers. This is 'money on the move'.

  All spending in the working capital area is called *Revenue Expenditure* or simply *Expenses.* The things that the expenses pay for are referred to as **current assets**.

So now we can draw a basic sketch of the money machine, something like the illustration below:

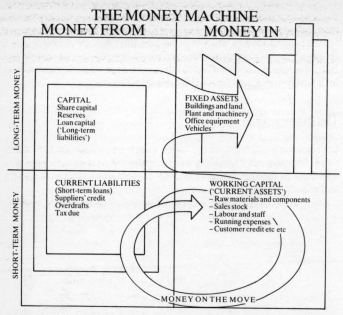

THE MONEY MACHINE

MONEY FROM · MONEY IN

LONG-TERM MONEY

CAPITAL
Share capital
Reserves
Loan capital
('Long-term
liabilities')

FIXED ASSETS
Buildings and land
Plant and machinery
Office equipment
Vehicles

SHORT-TERM MONEY

CURRENT LIABILITIES
(Short-term loans)
Suppliers' credit
Overdrafts
Tax due

WORKING CAPITAL
('CURRENT ASSETS')
– Raw materials and components
– Sales stock
– Labour and staff
– Running expenses \
– Customer credit etc etc

MONEY ON THE MOVE

In the money machine the money to the right of that central line always balances the money to the left. That's not because of the accountants' clever arithmetic, but because of the way the machine is made. All the money in fixed assets and working capital must have come from somewhere – either as capital or as short-term loans. If the figures don't balance, someone has forgotten something. It's impossible for the machine to be using more money than has actually been supplied by the combined sources. *The total of where the money has come from must always equal the total of where the money is invested.*

The horizontal line across the centre is another important division. It marks a time-period into the future of about a year. Money above the line doesn't generally move within that period – it's the more-or-less static money in the money machine. However, there *is* a tendency for the money to trickle slowly from above the line to below the line. Long-term loans eventually become short-term loans as their payment date approaches. And there's a gradual leaking of money from fixed assets into working capital – a process called 'depreciation' that we'll explain later.

The active part of the machine is below the line – the movement of the working capital in and out of the different stages of the operation. In any organisation, it moves in a cycle. Some organisations have short cycle-times: the money circulates quickly from buying in whatever the inputs are to the customer's payment for the output. Others have very long cycles, taking months or years to get from cash-into-raw-materials to products-into-cash. But before we consider the effects of the cycle's speed and other things, let's first get an idea of how the cycle itself works.

The money cycle

Let's take an example of a money machine – your pottery business, Moneypots Manufacturing Limited. It makes and supplies moneypots to your customers in sales-packs of a dozen as shown in the illustration.

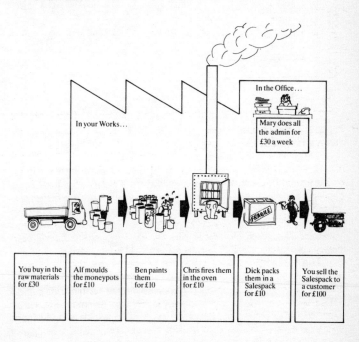

In the Office...

Mary does all the admin for £30 a week

In your Works...

| You buy in the raw materials for £30 | Alf moulds the moneypots for £10 | Ben paints them for £10 | Chris fires them in the oven for £10 | Dick packs them in a Salespack for £10 | You sell the Salespack to a customer for £100 |

The whole cycle of work, from raw materials arriving to a sales-pack going out, takes a week to complete. Let's look at what happens to £100 of your working capital during that week (suppose for the moment that every cost is paid on the dot as it's incurred):

This is where it goes. . .		*. . .and what's left*
Monday you buy raw materials	for £30	£70
Tuesday Alf moulds the pots	for £10	£60
Wednesday Ben paints them	for £10	£50
Thursday Chris fires them	for £10	£40
Friday Dick packs them	for £10	£30
Mary gets her weekly pay	of £30	
and arranges transport to the customer		
who pays you. . .		£100
Monday you buy raw materials	for £30	£70

So this is the week's cycle of your £100 – where it is when it isn't in actual cash in the bank:

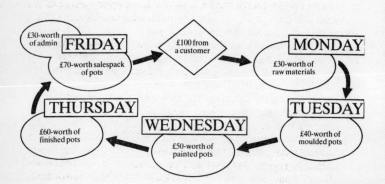

Now this is all very well, but you've spotted the snag, haven't you? The idea of the money machine is that each cycle produces money growth for you and Cousin Fred — for the owners. But where's the growth here? You've spent £100. You've got £100 back, and nothing left over it seems.

Ah, but this isn't the full story. The weekly cycle in your pottery isn't a once-a-week cycle. *Every day* you're buying £30-worth of raw materials. *Every day* Alf is making £40-worth of moulded pots. *Every day* Ben is converting them into £50-worth of painted pots . . . And *every day* a customer is paying you £100 for a sales-pack of finished pots. But you're paying Mary only *once a week*.

Mary is what is technically called an OVERHEAD. So to explain the cycle properly we now have to talk about the difference between 'overheads' and 'direct costs':

- **a direct cost** is a cost that's directly attributable to doing a particular piece of business — in your company, the cost of making a particular sales-pack of moneypots. *So it goes up and down in step with the amount of business you're doing.* If you don't do this piece of business, you don't have that cost. For instance in your business, the cost of raw materials: if you don't make the pots, you don't use the materials. The same for the pay of Alf, Ben, Chris and Dick. They get paid by the job — strictly on piecework. The more work for them to do, the more pay for them; if there's no work, they don't get paid that day (hardly a realistic assumption for employees in the real world, but accept it for the moment).

  You can *allocate* direct costs to the particular products they're in. It's possible to say 'this lump of cost is in that product there' (barring problems in keeping track of the things the costs have bought).

- **an overhead** is a cost you'll get whether or not you do a particular piece of business. *Generally, overheads stay the same whether the business goes up or down.* In Moneypots Manufacturing it doesn't matter if you do one order or five in a week, Mary still gets her £30 weekly pay. If there *is* only one order in a particular week you've got no profit. Your overhead (Mary's pay) has absorbed it all. But if you've got five orders in that week, her £30 paypacket can be divided between them. She adds only £6 to the cost of each order. With ten orders, her overhead would add £3 to each order.

  This doesn't mean that each order costs that much of Mary's time. You *apportion* her pay between your products in a somewhat arbitrary way — you can't allocate it as you can a direct cost.

  Another name for overheads is **indirect costs**.

There's a problem here with another pair of terms you'll often hear – **variable costs** and **fixed costs**. Direct costs are *always* variable, meaning they vary with the level of activity in the business. Overheads are occasionally variable too; *usually* they're fixed, meaning they *don't* vary with the activity level. That doesn't mean they're static. Rent and rates, insurance premiums – they may well change, but the changes won't have anything to do with the level of production or sales. In fact many accountants prefer to call them **period costs** because they depend more on the passing of time than anything else. The longer the period, the bigger the cost.

No cost is absolutely fixed. You *could* sack Mary and do the admin yourself. On the other hand if increasing business makes the admin too much for Mary to cope with, you might recruit Nancy for another £30 a week to assist her. You've doubled the admin overhead, but the amount of business may not have doubled. Where fixed costs do change they often change like this – going up and down in sudden steps. But otherwise, for small variations in production, they remain unchanged.

One further problem – *some costs are party variable, partly fixed*. Think of the telephone bill and its two components – the fixed rental, and the variable charge for the calls you've made. Another example is plant maintenance: even if the plant wasn't used there would be some regular maintenance needs for things like oiling and cleaning, but when it's in use the amount of maintenance and repair work rises. The more it's used, the bigger the maintenance cost. You can call such costs *semi-variable* or *semi-fixed* as you choose – for once the accountants haven't definitely decided.

So now let's redraw the money cycle to show the admin

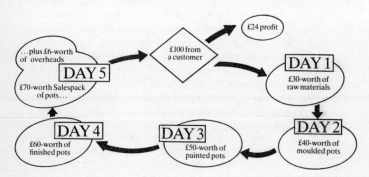

cost correctly shared between five orders per week. Whichever day of the week we take as the starting point of the cycle, it looks like the illustration on page 50.

Actually it's not quite accurate to call the £24 coming out of the cycle a 'profit'. That's because we've got quite a way to go yet before we can start calculating profit. But let it stand for now.

The working capital

We've been taking £100 of the working capital in Moneypots Manufacturing to illustrate what happens to it in the cycle of supplying an order. From the cycle you've just seen, you might spot that it's actually only £76 going round and round. That's the real amount involved. But let's not get too fussy about details. What we're interested in is the general principle on which the cycle works.

Now we'll try adding up the working capital you've got in total in the system. Remember, a fresh cycle starts every day. So every day you've got five cycles in progress, each one at a different stage. That's five orders on the go, each containing different amounts of your working capital. To see how much altogether, stop the action for a moment. What money is where?

Order 1 is in the shape of raw materials awaiting the start of manufacture } £30 in *raw materials*

Order 2 is £40-worth of moulded pots
Order 3 is £50-worth of painted pots
Order 4 is £60-worth of oven-fired pots } £150 in *work-in-progress*

Order 5 is a £70-worth pack of pots awaiting a customer – to which £6 overheads must be added } £76 in *finished goods*
_____
£256 total

As soon as the finished goods exit from the system and are converted into £100 cash, £76 of it goes back into the system. So the total is always £256.

No, that's not quite right. Now we have to go back to correct a fiction we've been using ever since this explanation started. "*Suppose*" we said "*that every cost is paid on the dot as it's incurred.*" Actually that doesn't happen. It can't happen.

There are delays built into every money machine – temporary traps that hold bits of working capital in suspense for short times before releasing it again. They, more than anything else, create the need for large amounts of working capital in every kind of business.

- **raw material stock**. Your suppliers deliver weekly, not daily. So you have to take one week's production requirements of raw materials at a time and put it in store until it's needed. That's 5 days' requirements at £30 a day = £150 worth of stock.

  Besides this, you've also found from experience that you need to keep a further one week's requirements as a buffer stock in case of emergencies. That's another £150 worth.

  So in total, at any point in time you have in store between £150 and £300 worth of raw material stock. Anyway, you've got to keep £300 of working capital available.

- **finished goods stock**. Although customer orders average one a day, they're not absolutely regular. You may get no orders for two days and then three in a day. To give the service your customers require, you find you have to keep a stock of finished goods – enough to cover a week's average sales. That's 5 days' production of £76-worth of goods per day = £380 worth of stock.

- **customers' credit**. To maintain good customer relationships you have to sell your goods on account. On average each customer takes six weeks to pay. That's 30 days' worth of production; £100 outstanding for each day = £3000 constantly owing to you.

  Actually this doesn't mean £3000 of working capital to fund the customer credit because it includes the profit of £720 (£24 a day for 30 days). The *costs* you've got to cover are 30 days at £76 per day = £2280. That's the amount of working capital in customer credit – more or less. Sometimes it's a bit above that, sometimes a bit below because customers aren't absolutely regular about the time they take to pay.

And don't forget the **work-in-progress** in our first listing of working capital. That's another £150-worth of part-finished goods constantly moving through the works.

Besides these money-traps, you'll also need to keep a certain amount of **cash in the bank** to pay the bills and wages as they become due and to absorb the ups-and-downs of trade. Say another £250 to £300 of ready money.

Now let's do some adding up. This is the picture of the amounts absorbed by the various money traps:

£300	in raw materials stock
£150	in work-in-progress
£380	in finished goods stock
£2280	in cost of goods sold awaiting payment
£290	cash in bank (say)
£3400	

So does that mean you're going to have something like £3400 tied up in working capital? Not exactly. There's one further point we're forgetting. *You* have a source of short-term funding yourself – your supplier. Just as you give credit to your customers, he gives credit to you. And that reduces the amount you have to provide from your other sources:

– **supplier's credit**. Your supplier gives *you* six weeks to pay *his* bills. At any point in time, you're being lent £900 of credit in six deliveries you still have to pay for. So you can deduct that to find what you have invested in working capital.

This gives a figure of about £2 500 working capital that's actually needed – but don't expect the figure to stay exactly the same as time goes on. Of course, for any particular point in time you can calculate it fairly precisely. But it won't stay at that figure – the next day it will be up or down to a greater or lesser extent. Perhaps you've had a delivery of raw materials. Maybe a bottle-neck in production has increased your work-in-process. Possibly a big customer has paid a rather overdue bill – or a sudden surge in business has increased the amount outstanding in customer credit. This is the point of the cash you keep at the bank, to cope with fluctuations like these.

The crucial point is whether you can pay your own bills on time. If you can't so that, no matter how good your incoming business looks, you're in trouble. You've run into the classic difficulty – the *cash flow* problem. In plain language, the organisation is skint. Now we'll look at the way this quite often happens.

Cash flow

Money and cash are not quite the same thing. What we've been describing in your moneypot business is a constant movement of money-values. Money moves when the raw material is turned into moulded pots. It moves when moulded pots become painted pots . . . The money inside the business moves constantly (apart from the pauses when it's caught in one of those money-traps).

Cash appears far less often. That's the point where the money comes out into the open – where it has to be paid into or out of the business. In fact, as we've described your business, cash is visible at just three points:

- the more-or-less £100 you receive daily from your customers £500 a week for the goods they received six weeks before.
- the weekly £150 you pay to your supplier for the materials you received six weeks earlier.
- the weekly £230 you pay your employees every Friday for their work that week: £50 each to Alf, Ben, Chris and Dick, £30 to Mary.

Whatever else happens to the money, the *timings* of those cash payments are vital. If the cash isn't there at the time it has to be paid out, a large spanner is thrown into the workings of the money machine.

Cash flow is affected by accidents in the business, big payments, persistent waste, sudden emergencies. It's also affected by quite normal developments – often in ways the managers concerned find surprising and unexpected. We'll use your pot-making business to explain some of these things.

First let's see what the normal pattern of cash-flow looks like. This is a picture of the weekly cash receipts and payments of the business when it's running at a steady five orders a week:

Weeks

	1	2	3	4	5	6	7	8	9	10
Receipts from customers	£500	£500	£500	£500	£500	£500	£500	£500	£500	£500
Payments to supplier	£150	£150	£150	£150	£150	£150	£150	£150	£150	£150
to employees	£230	£230	£230	£230	£230	£230	£230	£230	£230	£230
Cash flow plus or (minus)	£120	£120	£120	£120	£120	£120	£120	£120	£120	£120

£840

That's a nice positive cash flow of £120 a week your money machine is producing – the eventual source of profit you hope. Remember that figure and how it adds up – £240 in a fortnight, £480 in four weeks, £720 in six weeks, £840 in seven . . .

If the business suddenly falls to a lower level, what do you expect to happen to that cash flow? A smaller weekly figure

eventually, yes. But what about the *immediate* effect? Let's see. Assume your sales suddenly fall from five a week to four a week and settle at that lower level. What happens in the weeks following?

- for the next six weeks you're still getting £500 a week from customers. That's the result of the six weeks' credit they get. The receipts at the new £400-a-week level don't show up in the cash flow until week 7.
- payments to your supplier also reduce in six weeks' time. His deliveries are reduced from week 1, but this doesn't show up in the cash flow until week 7 – £30 less a week.
- labour payments drop immediately. Your works employees (Alf, Ben, Chris and Dick) are each now getting £10 less a week. That's a total of £40 less. (Mary still gets her usual £30 a week – fixed costs don't rise and fall with each variation in production.)

These aren't quite all the cash effects, but here's the picture so far. It'll give you a clue about the way things are working out:

	Weeks									
	1	2	3	4	5	6	7	8	9	10
Receipts from customers	£500	£500	£500	£500	£500	£500	£400	£400	£400	£400
Payments to supplier	£150	£150	£150	£150	£150	£150	£120	£120	£120	£120
to employees	£190	£190	£190	£190	£190	£190	£190	£190	£190	£190
Cash flow plus or (minus)	£160	£160	£160	£160	£160	£160	£ 90	£ 90	£ 90	£ 90

£1 050

Compare the cash flow here in the first seven weeks with the cash flow in the previous diagram. What would have been an £840 total at the old business level is apparently £1 050 now. Actually this understates the effect. There's even more cash floating out of the money machine from what's called *de-stocking*. For the reduced business you're now doing, you've overstocked both with raw materials and with finished goods:

– *finished goods stock*. It's there to cover a week's sales. That's now four orders, not five. You can reduce your stock by one case. So in week 1 you manufacture three cases instead of four. This has two effects: first, it reduces your labour requirements – your labour cost for the week is actually down to £150; secondly, it reduces your raw material requirements for the week by one unit.

– *raw material stock*. The regular deliveries are now four units a week instead of five. For week 1 we've already reduced that by a further one unit to make a delivery of three that week. But that's not all.

   Remember the buffer stock? That is to cover you for one week's production – five units at the old level, four now. You're overstocked by one unit of raw material. Reduce your week 1 delivery from your supplier by yet another unit. You want only *two* units that week. The reduction will show up in the cash flow as a smaller payment to the supplier in week 7.

So the actual cash flow looks like this:

					Weeks					
	1	2	3	4	5	6	7	8	9	10
Receipts from customers	£500	£500	£500	£500	£500	£500	£400	£400	£400	£400
Payments to supplier	£150	£150	£150	£150	£150	£150	£ 60	£120	£120	£120
to employees	£150	£190	£190	£190	£190	£190	£190	£190	£190	£190
Cash flow plus or (minus)	£200	£160	£160	£160	£160	£160	£150	£ 90	£ 90	£ 90

£1 150

The first seven weeks have actually produced a cash windfall of £1 150. Over that time the money machine has producd for you £310 more than you'd have had at the old five-sales-a-week level. The *immediate* effect of a drop in business is to make the money machine temporarily flush with ready cash!

Now can you reckon what happens when business *increases*? That's right – you run into a cash flow problem. A bigger business needs more working capital to finance it, and this rapidly shows up as a need for more cash to be pumped in.

Test the theory in Moneypots Manufacturing. A successful

sales drive increases your sales from five a week to a new steady
level of eight. Now you've got the destocking problem in reverse.
You have to increase both your finished goods stock and your
buffer stock of raw materials to match the new level. That means
manufacturing an extra three cases for stock. Let's say you do
this in week 1 – increasing your labour costs for that week, and
your raw materials requirements. Besides this, there's a further
increase in raw material deliveries necessary to top up the raw
materials buffer stock, *another* three units.

There's also an admin problem. Mary can't cope with the
extra work involved. You recruit Nancy to help – a further £30 a
week in the admin overhead.

So these are the cash flow effects:
- no increase in receipts from customers until week 7, then an
  extra £300 a week.
- payments to the supplier increase in week 7 – £90 more
  every week thereafter. Besides that, this particular payment
  has to include the stocking-up costs of the week 1 delivery –
  an extra six units, three for the finished goods stock, three
  for the raw materials buffer stock. That's an *extra* £180 in
  week 7.
- labour costs increase in week 1. There's a regular £120 a
  week more for your four works employees (£30 a week
  each). Also your admin overhead doubles – another £30 a
  week more. And don't forget the extra three orders in
  production in week 1 for your finished goods stock. That's a
  further £120 to your works labour that week.

Put all the figures together, and this is the cash flow in the weeks
following your sales success:

	Weeks									
	1	2	3	4	5	6	7	8	9	10
Receipts from customers	£500	£500	£500	£500	£500	£500	£800	£800	£800	£800
Payments to supplier	£150	£150	£150	£150	£150	£150	£420	£240	£240	£240
to employees	£500	£380	£380	£380	£380	£380	£380	£380	£380	£380
Cash flow plus or (minus)	£(150)	£(30)	£(30)	£(30)	£(30)	£(30)	0	£180	£180	£180

(£300)

Those bracketed cash flow figures are minus quantities (it's the
way accountants always show unfavourable figures). Over the
first seven weeks you've got a *negative* cash flow of £300.
Compare that with the plus £840 you'd have got at the old sales
level – you're well over £1 100 down. If you can find a way to
finance that cash flow deficit you're eventually into the oysters-
and-champagne country of a steady plus-£180 a week. Your *next*

seven weeks would produce a positive cash flow of £1 260. But will you get there? The immediate effect of an increase in business is often to make the money machine skint! It's a condition called 'over-trading'.

There's something that should by now be crystal-clear to you: *cash and profit aren't at all the same thing.* A business can be flush with cash when profits are actually falling – four orders a week wouldn't produce the profit that five orders would. On the other hand you can be strapped for cash when your profits are soaring. This is a vital point to appreciate about the money machine. Far more businesses go bust because of cash problems (what's technically called *insolvency*) than because of failure to make adequate profits.

For all that, no one can deny the importance of profit too. The cycle of the working capital explains how the profit is created, but it doesn't tell you how much you've made. That's because profit is what you get on the *total* of the capital employed in the business, not just on the working capital part of it. You have to look at what's happening to the money locked up in the fixed assets too.

Fixed assets

Let's suppose Moneypots Manufacturing Limited started with £10 000 capital – mostly from you and cousin Fred as shareholders. We've seen how some £2 500 of that is invested in working capital. The other £7 500 was used to buy equipment – Alf's moulding machine and Chris's oven. It's been put into fixed assets. So the next illustration shows the full picture of your money machine.

Actually that was the picture a year ago. The £7 500 in fixed assets represents what they cost you when you bought them new. But they're not worth £7 500 now. They're no longer new; they're not quite as up-to-date as today's machines; and they've had some wear from the use that's been made of them over the last year. They've DEPRECIATED in value.

Now think what that means – what's actually been happening. As Alf uses the moulding machine to mould a batch of pots, there's a tiny bit of wear on the machine. It becomes a tiny bit older. This reduces the machine's money-value by a small amount. Where has the money gone? It's now in that batch of moulded pots – instead of £40-worth they're actually worth £40-plus-a-bit. The same goes for Chris's oven. By the time the batch has been fired, the oven has lost a bit of its value too and the pots are worth £60-plus-a-bit-more. *The money in fixed assets is constantly leaking slowly into the*

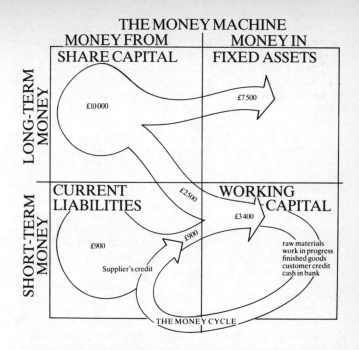

THE MONEY MACHINE

	MONEY FROM	MONEY IN
LONG-TERM MONEY	SHARE CAPITAL £10 000	FIXED ASSETS £7 500
SHORT-TERM MONEY	CURRENT LIABILITIES £900 Supplier's credit	WORKING CAPITAL £3 400 raw materials work in progress finished goods customer credit cash in bank

£2 500

£900

THE MONEY CYCLE

working capital area. The idea of depreciation is to represent this happening.

But how do you calculate the plus-a-bit on the cost of your pots? The difficulty is that no cash is changing hands. The other costs are easy to work out because cash *does* change hands: you have to pay your supplier for the raw materials for your pots; you have to pay Alf, Ben, Chris and Dick for their time, effort and skill that's in your pots. But no one pays anyone anything for the wear and ageing of your machines that's in the pots. You've got to go back to the cash that was originally paid for the machines and do some calculations based on that figure.

Whatever method you use, it's bound to be rather arbitrary. You start by estimating the working life of the machines in your business. Suppose you say the moulder and the oven will both give you ten years' service, and at the end of that time their value will be nil. Annually you're going to assume their value reduces by a tenth of the £7 500 you paid for them – £750 knocked off their value each year. So now a year after you bought them new, these fixed assets of yours are worth only £6750. In a year's time they'll be down to £6000 . . .

That £750 a year is coming into the working capital. It's another overhead just like Mary's pay. It's a fixed cost that doesn't depend on your production rate, so it has to be shared out between all the products made in a year – in just the same way that Mary's weekly £30 had to be shared between all the products made in a week. Let's assume your pottery is producing five sales-packs of moneypots per week, and it's doing that for fifty weeks in the year (the other fortnight is the annual shut-down). How much does this overhead add to each case? Now it's just a piece of simple arithmetic:
– £750 divided between 50 weeks = £15 per week
– £15 divided between 5 sales packs= £3 per pack
So now you've got a figure for the depreciation of your fixed assets that is contained in each finished case of pots.

You remember that earlier calculation of the cost per pack? Including Mary's overhead, we got a figure of £76 each. With the customers paying you £100 per case, we worked out a profit figure of £24 – though we did say at the time that it wasn't quite accurate to call it all profit. Now you can see why. That figure is too high. The cost to you of each sales-pack has to include that £3 share in the depreciation of your fixed assets. The cost is £79, not £76. Your profit is actually £21.

Profit

Profit is a vastly misunderstood word. It's commonly thought of as a pile of cash accumulated by each business and available to be paid out to the shareholders at the end of the year (less a bit for tax). This is what comes of confusing *money* and *cash*. Profit isn't spare cash. *Profit is growth in the size of the money machine.* In the same way, a loss would be a shrinkage in its size.

Take your pottery once again. Suppose after eight weeks' operation you wanted to check how much profit the business has earned so far. You started, remember, with your money machine turning over a steady five sales a week and looking like the following illustration.

The money machine: start date

	Money FROM	Money IN
Long-term money	SHARE CAPITAL £10 000	FIXED ASSETS £7 500
Short-term money	CURRENT LIABILITIES £900	WORKING CAPITAL £3 400

That was a total of £10 900 in the operation. What you are now going to count isn't how much more *cash* you've got. It's how much more the business is *worth* at the end of eight weeks irrespective of whether the money is cash in the company's bank account or work-in-progress in the factory or an amount owed by a customer. You add up the money in eight weeks' sales on the one hand (the income or 'revenue' of the business), and the money put into the goods you've parted with (the costs) on the other. It works out as shown in the illustration below.

Income and costs: weeks 1 to 8

Sales: 5 per week × 8 weeks
= 40 sales-packs sold at £100 each: £4 000 revenue

Cost of goods sold:

Direct costs { raw materials at £30 per sales-pack: £1 200

{ works labour at £40 per sales-pack: £1 600

Overheads { admin £30 weekly: £240

{ depreciation of fixed assets £15 weekly: £120

£3 160 costs

Profit: £840

But there are only a few pounds in the company's bank account – certainly nothing like £840. So where's the rest of the profit? Well, actually your business has increased from five to seven orders a week. Most of your profit is in the extra stock and extra customer credit the money machine is now financing. In round figures the extras add up like this:

	£
extra raw materials stock	60
extra work-in-progress	100
extra finished goods stock	150
extra customer credit	900
	1 210

Remember you're getting more credit from your supplier now because of the bigger raw material bills, so he is actually funding some £360 of the extra. But you still need £850 of extra working capital.

This is what your money machine looks like now:

The money machine: eight weeks later

	Money FROM	Money IN
Long-term money	SHARE CAPITAL £10 000 RESERVES (retained profit) £840	FIXED ASSETS £7 380
Short-term money	CURRENT LIABILITIES £1 260	WORKING CAPITAL £4 720

There's now a total of £12 100 in the operation, practically all of it being *used*. Certainly you couldn't take more than a hundred or so pounds cash out of it without starving the machine of money.

It's rather like what happens to a person's size as he grows up. Aged ten he's six stone. Aged twenty he's twelve stone. But that extra six stone isn't surplus that he could do without. For the human being what's an adequate weight at one stage is no longer adequate at another – the extra is necessary for survival. The same with a business. To survive in a world of inflation and shifting markets and changing technology, each money machine needs growth and profits just to remain in existence.

This isn't to deny that the shareholders should and do receive a dividend every so often. But in most companies, the largest part of the profits has already turned into so much extra capital being used in the operations of the money machine. To avoid hampering those operations by trying to extract the profit as cash, it's not unknown for a company to get a loan to pay the dividend!

This outline picture of the workings of the money machine is nearly complete. True, we've left out many of the finer points of detail that occur in any real company, but the fundamentals are there. There's just one extra feature to be added and a couple of general points about depreciation and its opposite – revaluation – to be made. The extra feature is an additional place the money may be in besides the two essential places, fixed assets and working capital:

Outside investments. They're more a wise precaution than an essential part of the money machine – a business equivalent to the spare petrol-cans strapped to the expedition's Landrover. The business has some of its money salted away in loans or in shares in other businesses or in other kinds of investment. The money is there for the future purchase of fixed assets perhaps, or to pay a future tax bill, or simply in case the working capital needs to be increased. Meanwhile it's getting the benefit of interest or capital growth elsewhere.

Are these investments a long-term or short-term place for the money? They could be either. If the money is likely to be needed in a hurry from time to time, it'll be stored in investments that can rapidly be turned into cash. But where the money is earmarked for a payment at a specified time well into the future, a long-term investment at a higher rate of interest is a better proposition.

Depreciation. Its purpose is to get a money-figure for the value that has passed from fixed assets – some equipment, say – into the sales the equipment has helped to make. *It isn't to find out what you could get for the equipment if you tried to sell it.*

Suppose you bought a delivery van for your pottery business and paid £6000 for it. You intend keeping it for four years by which time you reckon its resale value will be £2000. You decide to cost that shrinkage in your asset (the van) by £1000 a year. So in two years' time, the value of the van will be shown in your books as £4000. That figure represents its remaining value *in your business*, not its cash value in the market-place. If the business needed a sudden injection of cash, you couldn't expect to trundle the van around to your local secondhand van dealer and come back with £4000.

The point is that depreciation is a money convention, not a real movement of cash. It's based on the assumption that *the business will continue to keep and use its fixed assets*. With depreciation, there are only two points where the conventional money-values coincide with a real cash-value – when a fixed asset is bought and when it's eventually sold off at the end of its working life. At any other point its depreciated value is a hypothetical value to the business. That's all it can be, because there's no other way of estimating its *real* value in money terms.

63

Depreciation usually concerns fixed assets, but it can happen to current assets too. It is sometimes possible for current assets to depreciate below the value of money that was originally put into them. Think of a clothes shop left with a stock of last year's fashions. Think of a book publisher holding a lot of copies of what was a bestseller two years ago. As sales stock their value is now only a fraction of their cost. To that extent, the working capital has shrunk.

Revaluation. It's the opposite of depreciation – a way of acknowledging the fact that some assets actually increase in value as time passes – land and buildings particularly. Suppose you're a property owner having ten years ago bought a house for £30 000. If you put it on the market today you know it would fetch a lot more than that. So what do you set its value at? Perhaps £50 000? Or £60 000? If it's important for you to know – perhaps for insurance reasons – you might seek professional advice for a figure. You revalue your asset.

The same goes for the operations of the money machine. A business may have assets whose value has risen – and permanently risen (revaluation isn't for temporary and perhaps very transient gains in value). You may want to revalue them to keep the money picture reasonably accurate, or for some business purpose. But there's no compulsion to revalue. You're entitled to do it if you choose to, but you don't have to do it.

Like depreciation, revaluation doesn't concern only fixed assets such as land and property. Outside investments might be revalued from time to time, though there can be difficulties in doing this if the investments are, say, in companies without a Stock Exchange quotation. It may be very hard to assess the real value of some shares in those companies. Even materials or goods stocks might occasionally be revalued if prices have risen sharply since they were bought – although you'd probably have a battle with the accountants if you wanted to do this. Normal accountancy practice is to value stock at cost or market value *whichever is the lower*. It's depreciated if market value falls below cost, but there's a strong resistance to revaluing it however far the market value increases. Accountants are generally very cautious over claims that something is worth more than you actually paid for it.

Let's try and relate all of this to that picture of the money machine we drew earlier. We made the point at the time that that was a basic sketch. Now we can show some further pieces of the mechanism. We can fit the outside investments into the picture – the third place the money can be in – and show how some investments may be long term, others short term. We can also show the profit produced by the cycles of the working capital and where that profit goes – some out of the machine as dividends to the shareholders, the rest into the reserves as retained profit. Another point we can include too – the money that's slowly moving from fixed assets into the working capital area through the process called depreciation.

But what about revaluation? A property owned by your business increases in value – the money in it grows. You'll remember the rule that the totals to the left and right of the central division in the money machine must balance. There's now more money on the IN side, so it must be included somewhere in the FROM side. But where? What on earth can be its source? The shareholders haven't put it in; no one has lent the extra money; and it isn't retained profit because profit comes from the working capital, not directly from a fixed asset – your property.

The answer is the RESERVES. Now we have to explain the two kinds of reserve in the money machine. When we called retained profits 'reserves', we weren't misleading you but just not telling the full story, that's all. The reserve that's created by accumulating retained profits in the business the accountants call the *Revenue Reserve*. That's because their name for all the money moving around in the bottom half of the money machine is *revenue*, including the profit produced by the machine's cycles. But the reserves created by increases in the value of fixed assets is called the *Capital Reserve*.

So finally, let's see a complete picture of the money machine as shown in the following illustration.

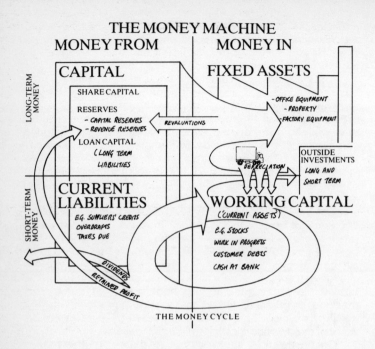

THE MONEY MACHINE

MONEY FROM	MONEY IN

CAPITAL   **FIXED ASSETS**

LONG-TERM MONEY

SHARE CAPITAL

RESERVES
- CAPITAL RESERVES
- REVENUE RESERVES

LOAN CAPITAL
(LONG TERM
LIABILITIES

REVALUATIONS

- OFFICE EQUIPMENT
- PROPERTY
- FACTORY EQUIPMENT

OUTSIDE INVESTMENTS
LONG AND SHORT TERM

DEPRECIATION

SHORT-TERM MONEY

CURRENT LIABILITIES

E.G. SUPPLIERS' CREDITS
OVERDRAFTS
TAXES DUE

WORKING CAPITAL
('CURRENT ASSETS')

E.G. STOCKS
WORK IN PROGRESS
CUSTOMER DEBTS
CASH AT BANK

DIVIDENDS

RETAINED PROFIT

THE MONEY CYCLE

3. Making sense of the accounts

Why should a business have to produce financial information at all? Yes, it's required by law, but there must be more to it than that. It can't just be a clever wheeze to provide jobs for accountants. Well, think of the different people who've got an interest in how a business is doing financially:

- *investors* want to know whether the business has good prospects for growth and future dividends.
- *lenders* need to feel confident about the security of any loans they might make.
- *tax authorities* demand evidence that profits and tax liabilities have been properly declared.
- *suppliers* may want proof that they can safely give credit.
- *a customer* may want assurance that the organisation will be a sound and reliable source of supply.
- *employees* may be concerned about job security and about fair distribution of the earnings they've helped to create.

... and the *managers* who are in the middle of all these various demands need to know what they're doing in financial terms. What are the money effects of the way they're running their operations? Of the decisions they take about new projects or investments? Of their methods of planning and controlling their work? Of the problems they are (or aren't) tackling? If they don't know what's happening to the money year by year, quarter by quarter, month by month, even week by week, it's only by accident they'll satisfy anyone – or even keep the business in existence.

Regular financial information about the condition of the money machine is obviously necessary for those who are supposed to be controlling it. But what sort of financial information? Let's begin with the two most basic financial statements – the *Profit and Loss Account*, and the *Balance Sheet*. You must have heard of them. But what do they tell you? They answer the two fundamental questions that anyone might ask who's considering an investment in a business – or in some Krugerrands or on a horse:

- what's the risk?
- what's the return?

69

Suppose you're at the races debating whether to place a bet. What do you need to know? Obviously the *odds* for one thing – that's your **return**, how your money will grow if the horse wins. The other thing is the *form* – where the horse finished in its previous races, the distance, the state of the ground, the weight it carried, the other horses it ran against . . . from which you estimate the likelihood of its winning this particular race, and so the **risk** of your money shrinking.

It's essentially the same in a business. How big a profit is the business making? That's the return you get – the equivalent to the punter's odds. The Profit and Loss Account tells you that. What's the risk you're taking if you invest? The Balance Sheet doesn't actually tell you that, no more than the form-book tells the punter. But it does give you clues on which you can make your own judgements of how sound the business is – much like the punter weighing up the chances on the basis of the form.

The first thing you have to hold on to is the difference between the two documents, and how they relate to each other. The Profit and Loss Account tells you the story of the growth or shrinkage of the money *over a period of time:* it's a summary of income and costs for that period and how they compare. The Balance Sheet gives you the financial picture of the business **at a point in time**: it's a snapshot of where the money is and where it's from at that point – a single frame from the continuing cine-film of the money machine. If you look at a succession of Balance Sheets and Profit and Loss Accounts for a business over several periods of time, what you're seeing is something like the illustration below. We'll take each in turn.

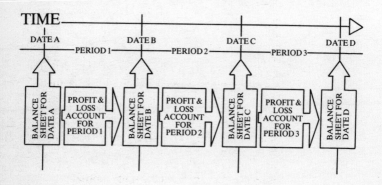

The profit and loss account

Don't lose sight of the key point: the Profit and Loss Account (commonly called the 'P-and-L') is about the moving part of the money in the money machine. So it's particularly concerned with the *working capital*. Its only interest in fixed assets is *depreciation*, the bit of their money that has leaked through into the working capital. It adds up the money in the sales made within the period – the income and the costs of those sales. If income exceeds costs, the business has grown – it's 'made a profit' as we all say. If it's the other way around, the business has shrunk – it's 'made a loss'.

The reckoning is done as soon as each period finishes:

Sales – what was the total value of products that customers actually bought in the period? This is the amount customers have been *invoiced* during the period, not the actual cash they've paid in that time. The P-and-L isn't a cash-flow statement.

Costs – what costs were in those products? Again this isn't cash paid out in the period. Some of the actual payments may be delayed. Some may have been made in advance – the price of the machines used to make the products, for instance. Remember the two kinds of costs:

(1) **Direct costs** in the products sold. If the business simply trades in the products as a retailer, they're the *purchase costs* of the products. If it's a manufacturing business, they're the *material and labour costs* in the products sold – which aren't the same as products *made* during the period. The costs must exclude materials and goods left in stock at the end of the period and the work-in-progress. What you're adding up in direct costs are the costs allocated to *the products customers have bought* in the period, and only those products.

(2) **Overheads** that properly belong to the period's sales – an apportioning of the fixed costs for things like admin, running expenses, management and staff salaries, rent and rates, depreciation etc during the period. There is often a lot of judgement involved in deciding how these costs are to be apportioned.

Notice we say 'apportioned', not 'allocated'. Direct costs can be firmly allocated. Each pound spent on materials and labour is there in a particular piece of merchandise. The only problem is to keep tabs on it. Overheads can only be apportioned – shared out between the various pieces of merchandise – using some rule-of-thumb method.

Profit – the result of deducting Costs from Sales.
(or loss)

Actually you've already seen a simple example of a P-and-L – the income and costs statement on page 61. The accountants work these things out in considerable detail. For an example of the sorts of things you might see, imagine we're looking at the annual accounts of Moneypots Manufacturing Limited some years on – now an established company. Let's suppose we're just into the year 1990, so the accounts are for the last year, January to December 1989. Over the year you've sold £700 000 worth of goods.

The first part of the calculation is called the '*Trading Account*', (though actually it's all part of the P-and-L). Its object is to establish what you've spent in buying the stock-in-trade you've sold – or in making it in your case. There are many, many different ways of laying the figures out, but in principle this is the way you do it:

– you begin by calculating the value of raw materials used by the factory during the period. There's a complication here because you can't simply take the costs of the materials you've *bought* during the year. The factory drew its materials from the material stock you keep. So you have to add up what was there originally (the 'opening stock') and how much was bought in, and then subtract what's left at the end (the 'closing stock'). This tells you what was actually used:

Raw materials		
	opening stock	£ 23 000
	purchases	193 000
		216 000
	less closing stock	26 000
Cost of raw materials used		190 000

– next you add in the cost of the production labour: direct labour, that is – the successors of Alf, Ben, Chris and Dick on the factory floor. You *exclude* the pay of people like managers and supervisors and maintenance engineers and production control clerks and anyone else who wasn't directly engaged in making the products:

Direct labour	£150 000
	340 000

This last figure is called the *Prime Cost* of production – the material and work that actually went into making products during the period (irrespective of whether the products have yet been sold).

– now to get the total cost of making the products, the overheads of the Production Department have to be added in:

Production overheads	indirect labour	£12 000
	management	40 000
	electricity, gas etc	7 000
	plant maintenance	13 000
	depreciation of factory and plant	8 000
		80 000

| Add that to the Prime Cost . . . | 340 000 |
| | 420 000 |

. . . which was the total production cost of the goods made. Now to find out what was put into the finished goods stock, we have to allow for the work-in-progress, the semi-finished stuff still in the factory.

Work-in-progress is another kind of stock – like the raw materials, but half way to turning into finished goods stock. So we've got to calculate the difference between the work-in-progress at the start of the period and the work-in-progress at the end of that period, like we did with the raw materials just now:

Work-in-progress	opening stock	£ 4 000
	closing stock	6 000
		(2 000)

The brackets show this has to be *deducted* from the Prime Cost to get the value of goods going into finished stock. It's a *minus* quantity, but do you see why? It means that £2 000 of the Prime Cost has gone into extra half-finished goods in the factory, not into finished goods in the finished goods store. It was actually £418 000-worth of goods that reached the next stage.

– so now we can calculate the production costs in the goods actually sold – which aren't the same thing as the goods put into the finished goods stock. There's a similar calculation for the stuff entering and leaving the finished goods stock as there was for raw materials:

Finished goods	opening stock	£ 28 000
	received from Production	418 000
		446 000
less closing stock		30 000
Cost of goods sold		416 000

If yours were a retail business, this is where your Trading Account would begin. Instead of a 'received from Production' cost, you'd have a 'stock purchase' cost for the period.

- at this point we can work out the *Gross Profit* – the difference between the cost of the goods sold and the price the customers have paid for them, the Sales figure:

Sales	£700 000
less cost of goods sold	416 000
Gross profit	284 000

This isn't the actual profit yet because it includes yet more costs that have to be taken out. There are the costs of running the company's offices – Mary and all her co-workers in the Admin Department. Besides this, you now have a Sales Department which costs money. There was also Aunt Mabel's loan that you have to allow for the interest on . . .

- so now we get to the real profit, the *Net Profit*. This final stage in calculating it and in saying what's to be done with it is what is actually called the P-and-L in many companies, as shown below.

Moneypots Manufacturing Limited

PROFIT AND LOSS ACCOUNT FOR YEAR ENDED 31 DECEMBER 1989

		£	£	£
Gross profit				284 000
Selling expenses	sales force pay	60 000		
	sales office pay	22 000		
	travel expenses	21 000		
	depreciation of cars	5 000		
			108 000	
Admin overheads	management and staff pay	124 000		
	office expenses	20 000		
	depreciation of office equipment	2 000		
			146 000	
Loan interest			2 000	
total deductions before tax				256 000
Net profit before tax				28 000
Tax				8 000
Net profit after tax				20 000
Dividend				18 000
Retained profit to Revenue Reserve				2 000

. . . and at last we've reached the 'real' profit — as far as any profit figure is a real one. That £700 000-worth of sales in the year has earned just £20 000 after tax, nearly all of which you've decided to pay out to the shareholders as dividends. You're retaining only £2 000 as growth in the business.

A year isn't the only period a P-and-L can cover of course. You could do one for each quarter if you wanted — or even for each month. In fact this is a key point. *Over what period do you measure profit and loss?*

The important period is the *trading cycle*. How long does it take to get the seasonal ups and downs of sales to cancel each other out? In many if not most businesses that's a full year. Anything less is too short to iron out the regular peaks and valleys in the pattern of trade. Even if the law didn't demand annual accounts, a year would still be the right period in most types of company to give a realistic picture of the growth or shrinkage of working capital.

Of course, managers usually want P-and-L accounts for shorter periods within the year — perhaps quarterly, perhaps monthly. But these accounts can't represent the full picture. If you were in the Christmas tree business, the fact that the P-and-Ls for eleven months of the year showed a crashing loss would hardly surprise you! Your costs continue throughout the year, but all the income to set against them comes in just one month. The real point of a short-stage account is to compare it with the same period last year and the year before . . . It might be worth knowing in advance of the end-of-year P-and-L that a cost is rising far enough to jeopardise the eventual profit, so that you can do something about it fast.

There can be a problem the other way: for some things a year might be too short a period. The basic idea of the P-and-L is that it relates the sales of the period to the cost of those sales. But suppose some expenses *this* year are for the benefit of sales *next* year and the year after? Or what if some costs that properly belong to this year's sales aren't going to appear for several years to come? Take some examples:

- a project has been started to develop a revolutionary new product. It will take two years to complete. The development work is costing money this year, but there won't be any sales to relate to those costs until the product reaches the market two years from now. How can the costs of the project be treated in this year's P-and-L?
- the new product reaches the market, and a heavy advertising campaign is run to launch it. There will be some initial market resistance and you don't expect the really big pay-off to begin until the *next* year's sales. True,

the advertising will create some sales this year, but the important point is its carry-over effect into future years. Is it reasonable to put the full cost of the campaign into this year's P-and-L?
- a big programme of management training is to be run during this year. The immediate pay-off from improved management methods is likely to be small. The real point is to develop the management abilities needed to manage the company growth and acquisitions that are planned for the next five years. Should this year's profits bear the full brunt of the cost of the training programme?

The only answer the conventional year-to-year system of accounting can offer is to treat such a cost in the same way as the cost of buying some equipment for the factory. The development project, the advertising campaign, the training programme is regarded as a fixed asset. Its cost is *'capitalised'*, as the accountants say – meaning that it's treated as capital expenditure (which doesn't appear in the P-and-L) rather than revenue expenditure (which does). Now the cost can be spread over the years the organisation is getting value from it. Just like the cost of a production machine or a delivery vehicle, it passes little by little through into future P-and-Ls in the form of *depreciation*. (In fairness we must also say that accountants don't like the idea of capitalising the costs of intangible things because it's open to so many fiddles.)

If the delayed returns from the intangible assets like these create a problem, an even greater one is caused by delayed costs – costs that rightfully belong to this year's sales but

76

won't appear until next year or the year after or the year after that ... Sometimes they are a long-postponed result of practices the organisation reckoned acceptable (or that it kept quiet about) at the time, but whose chickens came home to roost rather unpleasantly afterwards. The time period can be very long indeed:

- In 1930 a company started dumping toxic waste in a disused canal. When dumping ceased, the site was covered over and disposed of. The company gave no information at all about the actual constituents of the waste apart from assurances that they were a hazard only if they were physically touched or swallowed. As the years passed, families living in the area began to suffer severe health problems which were eventually traced to leakages of the dumped chemicals. In the 1980s the company was forced to pay heavy damages.

    The damages were of course a cost on the company's operations – but to what periods' operations did that cost relate? Obviously not to the time when the damages were paid, but to the time when the practices were being followed that led to the damages being imposed. The costs actually began to accumulate when the company began its dumping, so should have been matched against the sales of that period and the following periods while dumping continued. The fact that fifty years passed between the start of the dumping and the payment doesn't alter the principle: to work out the profit of a period, you have to deduct from the sales revenue the *full* cost of those sales. To the extent that the company failed to report the potential costs of its waste disposal practices, it overstated its profits in those early years.

You might argue that such long-term predictions of eventual costs are quite impossible to do in practice. Certainly it would have been a prodigious feat to anticipate costs in the 1930s that wouldn't become payable until the 1980s. But in principle there's no difference between this and estimating the depreciation to apply in a particular period on a very, very long-lived fixed asset. Judgement is involved in both. The difference is its difficulty. But you're just as much guessing the future if you exclude such costs as if you include them (or at least an estimate of what they might be once it's clear there's an actual or potential human or environmental impact).

These problems of delayed returns and delayed costs are ones that the system of annual P-and-Ls is poorly designed to handle. Yet most accountants prefer to ignore the problems. Even though the only results a current research project can produce will be in the earnings of future years, the normal accountancy practice is to show its costs as current expenditure in this year's P-and-L.

Managers can't afford to be so short-sighted – particularly senior managers. Where they decide to spend this year on intangibles like advertising or training or improved management selection whose benefits will be felt mainly or entirely in future years, they know they have to interpret the bare figures in the P-and-Ls accordingly. To the extent of the spending, this year's P-and-L is going to understate the profits, and future P-and-Ls (which get the revenue benefits without bearing the costs) will overstate the profits. On the other hand, if managers are considering some practice that will increase sales or reduce costs this year, but which is likely to have bad social or environmental consequences – and quite possibly cost the company a packet in the future – do they reckon its effect beyond the current P-and-L? Could those short-term gains turn out eventually to be bogus, costing the company heavily in future lost reputation and lost sales or even putting its very survival at risk?

The point is that a profit can never be an absolute, precise amount of money. There are too many variables, too many judgements involved in reckoning exactly what costs attach to each lump of revenue earned. Every profit a business declares is to some extent the opinion of the managers running the business.

The *managers*, not the accountants. It's managers, not accountants, who have to make judgements about stock – its condition, its saleability, its value. It's managers, not accountants, whose assessments are the basis of depreciation – assessing the life of a machine, its scrap value, how its depreciation should be spread. It's managers, not accountants, who reckon the way overheads should be apportioned among the goods and services provided to the customers. It's managers, not accountants, who make the decisions about company practices or policies that may contain hidden long-term costs. *And all these managerial judgements directly affect profits.* The accountant calculates the figures that result from the judgements; he may help the managers to define what judgements they have to make. But he is in no position to make the judgements for them.

The balance sheet

In fact you already know the basic shape of the balance sheet. It's the picture of the money machine we were drawing in the last chapter – the way the machine looked on a given date, how much money it contained from where and what the money was in. The structure of a balance sheet is shown in the following illustration.

The balance sheet		
	Money FROM	Money IN
Long-term money	CAPITAL Shares Reserves Loans	FIXED ASSETS Property Equipment etc.
		INVESTMENTS
Short-term money	CURRENT LIABILITIES Suppliers credit Overdrafts Taxes due etc.	CURRENT ASSETS (WORKING CAPITAL) Stock Customers' credit Cash in bank etc.

The sources of capital and short-term money, the amount in fixed assets and the various parts of the working capital – they're all there, all frozen at a given point in time. The actual layout of the sheet in a particular company might differ from this, but in one way or another these are the things it tells you.

The next illustration shows the balance sheet for Moneypots Manufacturing Limited on 31 December 1989 – the moment the period covered by the P-and-L on page 73 finished. Let's look at it to see what it tells you:

Moneypots Manufacturing Limited
BALANCE SHEET AT 31 DECEMBER 1989

Capital	£	Fixed assets	Cost or valuation	Accumulated depreciation	Net
Share capital			£	£	£
100 000 issued shares of £1 each, fully paid	100 000				
Reserves					
Capital reserve	30 000				
Revenue reserve	57 000	Factory property	60 000	8 000	52 000
Loan Capital		Factory plant	30 000	20 000	10 000
8% debentures 1994/5	25 000	Office equipment	12 000	5 000	7 000
		Sales force cars	30 000	14 000	16 000
		TOTAL FIXED ASSETS	132 000	46 000	86 000
TOTAL CAPITAL	212 000				

Current liabilities	£	Current assets		£	£
Creditors	39 000		Raw material	26 000	
Accruals	1 000	Stock	Work-in-progress	6 000	
Interest	2 000		Finished goods	30 000	
Tax	8 000				
Dividend declared	18 000				
TOTAL CURRENT LIABILITIES	68 000	Total stock			62 000
		Debtors			117 000
		Prepayments			2 000
		Cash at bank:			13 000
		TOTAL CURRENT ASSETS			194 000

TOTAL MONEY	280 000	TOTAL ASSETS	280 000

A lot of the picture should be fairly familiar to you. There are you and cousin Fred and the other shareholders between you owning the *SHARE CAPITAL* and the *RESERVES*, all £187 000 of it. Aunt Mabel's *CAPITAL LOAN* is there in the £25 000-worth of debentures earning a steady 8% a year. Debentures are contracts the company enters into for its long-term borrowings, undertakings to pay the stated rate of interest and to repay the principle by the time specified – whether as a lump sum or by instalments. In this case the undertaking is to repay the lump sum at some time in 1994 or 1995. Meanwhile you pay 8% interest to the debenture-holders each year – the £2 000 you've seen in the P-and-L on page 73.

A couple of years ago you made a shrewd purchase of a property for your factory – bought it for £30 000 and it's worth double that now. Under *FIXED ASSETS* is the figure it's now valued at in your books and you'll see the gain in your capital under *capital reserve*. The *revenue reserve* is the total amount of retained profit the business has accumulated over the years.

The *FIXED ASSETS* show three figures for each type of asset. First what the assets cost to buy (apart from the property of course, which is there at your revalued figure). Secondly the accumulated depreciation – the total reduction in their money value since then, which has gradually passed into successive years' P-and-Ls under the headings of *Production overheads*, *Selling expenses* and *Admin overheads*: you can see this year's apportionments in the Trading Account and the P-and-L on page 73 again. The last figure, the net value, says how much was left in each asset on 31 December – the cost or valuation, minus the depreciation.

The *CURRENT LIABILITIES* are the bills the company owed on 31 December that have to be paid before *next* 31 December. In practice they've all got to be paid long before then of course. Some might even be paid the next day (a balance sheet for 1 January could well look slightly different). Among them are your suppliers – your 'creditors' in the jargon. There's also the tax bill, the interest you owe Aunt Mabel for the year, and the £18 000 dividend you've decided you and cousin Fred can take out of the £20 000 profit after tax (all shown in the P-and-L). The other £2 000 profit is there in the £57 000 of your revenue reserve.

The word **accruals** might well puzzle you. It's the jargon for owings that pile up over a period. The electricity account is a good example. You're using electricity continually, but you pay for it *in arrears* when the quarterly bill arrives. It's a cost that gradually accumulates like the slow rise of the water-level in a cistern up to the point where the cistern empties. It then begins to accumulate again. At a particular point in time – the balance sheet date – the level has risen so far, and even though you don't have the bill you can make a pretty good estimate of what's owing. The accruals figure is that estimate. This one includes not only electricity but also gas, water and telephones – all typical examples of charges that accrue steadily through time.

CURRENT ASSETS you'll remember is the term for the things you've got your *working capital* in. You'll see the stock figures are the same as the figures given in the Trading Account as 'closing stock'.

One term, **debtors**, we haven't used before. It's what we called 'customer credit' earlier – to your customers it's credit, but from your point of view it's their debt to you. Remember which way around the two words go, because it's easy to get confused by them:

- creditors are people *you owe* money to
- debtors are people who *owe you* money

There's also another new term, **prepayments**. They're the reverse of accruals – payments you make *in advance* for something that is gradually used up over the following period. An insurance premium is an example. You pay an annual premium now, and in six months' time you've still got half its value left. Other examples are rent and rates. Each payment buys a certain amount of value that reduces through time. A prepayment figure in a balance sheet shows the unexpired portion of the value.

Be prepared for one thing: balance sheets aren't always laid out in the way we've illustrated. It's quite common to start with the Fixed Assets, then to show the Current Assets and deduct the Current Liabilities from them, and finally to show the Capital. The balance sheet on the next page means exactly the same as the last one.

Moneypots Manufacturing Limited		
BALANCE SHEET AT 31 DECEMBER 1989		
FIXED ASSETS		
		£
At cost or valuation:		132 000
less Accumulated depreciation		46 000
Net		86 000
CURRENT ASSETS		
	£	
Stock	62 000	
Debtors	117 000	
Prepayments	2 000	
Cash	13 000	
	194 000	
less *CURRENT LIABILITIES*		
Creditors	39 000	
Accruals	1 000	
Interest	2 000	
Tax	8 000	
Dividend declared	18 000	
	68 000	126 000
Net assets		212 000
CAPITAL		
Share capital		100 000
Capital Reserve		30 000
Revenue Reserve		57 000
Loan Capital (8% debentures 1994/5)		25 000
		212 000

All this explains what's in the balance sheet but it doesn't explain 'so what?' That's a question that usually requires more than one balance sheet to answer, so that you can begin to see patterns and detect trends particularly. What do you notice when you look at the Moneypots Manufacturing balance sheet for 31 December 1989 (which you've already seen) alongside the figures for the year before? To avoid a lot of noughts, we have given the figures in thousands this time.

MONEYPOTS MANUFACTURING LIMITED
Balance sheets at 31 December 1988 and 1989

Capital	'88	'89	Fixed assets	Cost or valuation		Accumulated depreciation		Net	
	£'000	£'000		'88 £'000	'89 £'000	'88 £'000	'89 £'000	'88 £'000	'89 £'000
Share capital	100	100	Factory property	30	60	4	8	26	52
			Factory plant	30	30	16	20	14	10
Reserves: capital	–	30	Office equipment	10	12	3	5	7	7
Revenue	55	57	Sales-force cars	15	30	9	14	6	16
Loan Capital (8% debentures)	–	25		85	132	32	47	53	85
	155	212							

Current liabilities			Current assets		
	'88	'89		'88	'89
	£'000	£'000		£'000	£'000
Creditors	44	39	Raw materials	23	26
Accruals	1	1	Work-in-progress	4	6
Debenture interest	–	2	Finished goods	28	30
			Stock total	55	62
Tax	14	8	Debtors	107	117
Dividend declared	20	18	Prepayments	2	2
	79	68	Cash at bank	17	13
				181	194
Total Capital Liabilities	234	280	Total Assets	234	280

Now you can begin to see how the balance sheets are connected by the P-and-L. Take profit for instance. The P-and-L for Moneypots Manufacturing's trading year gave the retained profit as £2000. Can you find it in the two balance sheets? Look at the figures for the revenue reserve for the *two* years – it's the difference between them. Not a big difference. Is too much being taken out in the dividends? There might be some evidence for this in the fact the company has had to raise a capital loan during the year. There wasn't any loan money there a year before! And perhaps that explains the property revaluation. Revaluations are sometimes done to improve the look of the balance sheet before an approach to the money markets or to offset a write-off of some other assets in the sheet.

What else do you notice? The *direction* in which the figures have moved, and how far? You've bought some new assets in the year – £15 000-worth of cars for the sales force, and a bit of equipment for the office. You're actually taking less credit from your suppliers than you had a year ago – but with a bigger stock of raw materials. That might be something to investigate, particularly when the debtors figure (the credit you're giving to your customers) is climbing.

There are several obvious things like these you might spot. But other things won't be so obvious until you start doing some calculations on the figures to get some information out of them. Among the most useful calculations to make are *ratios*.

Ratios

By themselves, the figures in balance sheets and P-and-L accounts can provide only *data*, not *information*. It's a distinction you're probably aware of even if you haven't ever put it that way before. Data are facts and figures that are meaningless by themselves. You can look at them and ask "so what?" and you've no answer to the question:

- "Moneypots Manufacturing made £28 000 net profit before tax in 1989" – "so what?"
- "Moneypots Manufacturing had an income of £70 000 in 1989" – "so what?"
- "Moneypots Manufacturing had total assets of £280 000 on 31 December 1989" – "so what?"

By itself each statement leaves the question in the air. But if you put the statements together and compare one with another, you do start to get some significant information. The comparisons that produce information out of the cold statistics are mainly ratios of one sort or another. For the managers of a business, two sorts are particularly important – profitability ratios and liquidity ratios.

Profitability ratios

Is £28 000 net profit good or bad? It could be either. If it took £10 000 000 sales and £1 000 000 of assets to make it, it would be ridiculously low. But if the total sales had been £50 000 on a £25 000 asset base, it would be obscenely high. Profit isn't the real point. Profit*ability* is what tells you how well a business has performed, and profitability is always a ratio, a comparison between two figures. For instance:

Profit v. sales. This is the *profit margin* of the business during the year:

profit	v.	*sales*
£28 000	:	£700 000

You can then reduce it to simpler terms. You can work it out as a percentage and say that profit is 4% of sales, in other words that every £100 of sales produced £4 of profit. Or you can calculate the ratio and call it 1 : 25, which is to say that every £1 of profit took £25 of sales to make it. You can then compare that profit margin with the margin for previous years to see how the ratio is moving – is it getting better or worse? You can also relate it to the general business scene to see how you reckon it *should* have moved, and what you think it *ought* to be now.

Profit v. assets. This is generally called the *profitability* of the business to distinguish it from the profit margin.

profit	v.	*assets*
£28 000	:	£280 000

In percentage terms, your profit was 10% of your assets. As a ratio that is 1 : 10. And again you can relate that to previous years' ratios and perhaps to the performance of similar businesses. Knowing the business, do you consider that an adequate rate of return?

Actually many companies prefer to calculate profitability on their *capital employed* rather than total assets. Some even limit that to *shareholders' capital*, leaving out the loan capital under the heading of long-term liabilities. In your business, the first method would compare your profit with £212 000 and the second would compare it with £187 000. Obviously these ratios would be rather different:

| profit: capital employed | 1 : 7.7 or 13% |
| profit: share capital | 1 : 6.7 or 15% |

We've quoted both percentage and ratio figures because you could calculate the ratios either way. In practice of course, you choose one and stick to it – probably percentages in talking about profit.

Should profitability be calculated on total assets or on capital employed? Return on Capital Employed ('ROCE' as it's often called) is the popular answer. But there's a sound case for preferring Return on Total Assets, on the argument that the managers of a company are responsible for the lot in any case, not just the part the shareholders are providing. In the actual running of the company it doesn't much matter how the resources are financed – whether by shareholders or by lenders long- or short-term.

The two kinds of ratios we've mentioned are at the head of a whole range of inter-related ratios, each one a useful indicator of some aspect of a business's performance. In combination they can often reveal strengths and weaknesses in the business or in particular parts of it. They are linked to each other in a pyramid of subdivisions, as illustrated in the next diagram.

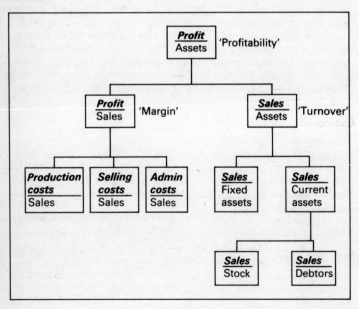

Let's explain how the pyramid works. Take the first three ratios: profit to assets, profit to sales (the two we've illustrated already) and sales to assets – the 'Turnover' (the amount of sales generated by the total assets over the year, how many times the assets can be said to have 'turned over' in that time). The first one, the Profitability ratio, can be broken down into the two ratios below – Margin and Turnover. In other words:

$$\frac{profit}{sales} \times \frac{sales}{assets} = \frac{profit}{assets}$$

When the two are multiplied together, the sales component gets cancelled out. Try it with the Moneypots Manufacturing figures:

$$\frac{£28\,000\ profit}{£700\,000\ sales} \times \frac{£700\,000\ sales}{£280\,000\ assets} = \frac{£28\,000\ profit}{£28\,000\ assets}$$

In percentages the calculation translates into this:

margin		turnover		profitability
4%	of	250%	equals	10%

The point of relating the ratios like this is that any given profitability ratio can be achieved by many different combinations of margin and turnover. Different kinds of business can produce the same profitability with very different margins. One business may have a high margin coupled with a low turnover, another a low margin with a high turnover. The first is, say, an engineering manufacturer with expensive production plant and a lot of money tied up in slow-moving stocks and work-in-progress. Turnover inevitably would be low, but this would be counter-balanced by high profit margins – perhaps something like this:

Engineering manufacturer

margin		turnover		profitability
40%	of	37.5%	equals	15%

The other business is a discount store which operates on very small profit margins, but achieves a high turnover through its fast-moving stock and by keeping its investment in fixed assets low – avoiding frills like delivery vans and expensive shop fittings. The same profitability might be achieved like this:

Discount store

margin		turnover		profitability
5%	of	300%	equals	15%

In the pyramid below these ratios, the subdivisions on each side investigate the detailed make-up of the ratios above them.

The *margin* side, on the left, contains the ratios you get from the P-and-L. Profit is sales less costs. So the three ratios below show the proportion of sales income absorbed by each of the main cost-producers in Moneypots Manufacturing. If the profit margin is falling because of escalating costs, these ratios will point out where the problem is.

In your P-and-L, the three ratios are:

$$\frac{Production\ costs}{Sales} \qquad \frac{£418\,000}{£700\,000} \qquad = \qquad 59.7\%$$

$$\frac{Selling\ costs}{Sales} \qquad \frac{£108\,000}{£700\,000} \qquad = \qquad 15.4\%$$

$$\frac{Admin\ costs}{Sales} \qquad \frac{£146\,000}{£700\,000} \qquad = \qquad 20.9\%$$

With knowledge of these ratios in previous years and of the general nature of the business, you'd be able to spot whether any of these suggested a problem, or whether there was a trend that warranted closer investigation.

The **turnover** side of the pyramid analyses how well the assets are being used in the business. So these ratios relate balance sheet figures to the sales figure in the P-and-L.

Sales v. fixed assets. This ratio indicates how the capacity of plant, equipment and property are being used. At least, it will show a trend towards under-using these assets – or, to put it another way, if there is too much money invested in fixed assets for the amount of business being done. It might on occasions hint at the opposite – that a company is trying to conduct its business with antiquated and clapped-out equipment which by now has depreciated to almost nil value. Of course, you'd need to know the business to draw a conclusion like that, but the ratio might have provided a clue.

The ratio from the Moneypots Manufacturing balance sheet figure is:

$$\frac{sales}{fixed\ assets} \qquad \frac{£700\,000}{£86\,000} \qquad = \qquad 814\%$$

. . . which says that each £100 of the net fixed assets generated £814 of sales.

Sales v. current assets. This is about the money in the moving part of the money machine of course – the working capital. How well is that being used to generate sales? For Moneypots Manufacturing the ratio is:

$$\frac{sales}{current\ assets} \qquad \frac{£700\,000}{£194\,000} = 361\%$$

Each £100 circulating in current assets created £361 of sales during the year. By itself perhaps that doesn't tell you a lot, but the two sub-ratios can be informative:

Sales v. stock. 'Stock' includes all the different kinds of things you can count as stock. What you're interested in is the speed at which they move through the business from the point at which they came in as raw materials to the time they leave as sales. In Moneypots, the ratio is:

$$\frac{sales}{stock} \qquad \frac{£700\,000}{£62\,000} = 1129\%$$

Each £100 of money in stock produced £1129 sales.

Actually this isn't a very good way of getting at *stock turnover* – the times the stock turned over in the year. This ratio is an inaccurate way of measuring it because sales includes your gross profit but the stock figure doesn't – it's a *cost* figure. The percentage suggests your stock turned over about eleven times in the year, but this isn't actually so. You get a better measure from *cost of goods sold* rather than sales – the cost of what you have in stock against the cost of the stuff that's gone through:

$$\frac{cost\ of\ goods\ sold}{stock} \qquad \frac{£418\,000}{£62\,000} = 674\%$$

Your stock actually turned over rather more than six-and-a-half times in the year.

If this calculation produced a ratio you reckoned was too low, you'd then start looking in more detail at your front-end stocks of raw materials and components, your work-in-progress and how efficiently the production processes are getting it through, your finished goods stock: do you need to carry so much? Could you economise in stock-holdings without harming the efficiency of the business or its marketing?

Sales v. debtors. This shows how quickly customers are settling their accounts. The Moneypots Manufacturing ratio is:

$$\frac{sales}{debtors} \qquad \frac{£700\,000}{£117\,000} = 600\%$$

Your debtors are just one sixth of your sales. In other words your customers are taking on average one-sixth of a year, two months to pay their accounts.

If you calculate these ratios regularly from a company's P-and-Ls and balance sheets, you can watch for trends, detect the early signs of problems, make changes before you're in real trouble. But drawing conclusions like these does require knowing how the company is being run, and something about the industry and the markets in which it is operating. Uninformed opinion based merely on ratios isn't likely to be worth much.

Liquidity ratios

The 'liquidity' of a company is its ability to pay its way in the short term. So what we are looking at in these ratios are the financial safety-margins on which the firm operates: how easily can the company meet its debts to people like suppliers, the taxman and so on – its current liabilities in other words?

The *balance sheet* provides the data for these ratios, which all relate current liabilities to current assets or different portions of them. It's a question of how quickly the current assets can be turned into cash. Obviously, some are further away from that point than others. In Moneypots Manufacturing, your raw material stock is furthest from cash. It has to go right through the processes of being issued to production, being used in manufacture, being held in finished goods stock, getting sold to a customer and waiting for the customer to pay the bill before it turns back into ready money. Work-in-progress is slightly nearer cash, finished goods nearer still, and customer debts the last stage before cash actually appears. So each of these is a stage closer to liquidity – the cash itself. There's also a totally liquid asset in your cash in the bank, of course.

These are general principles, not rules. Sometimes some raw material may be very saleable just as it is. And you've also to consider the company's *outside investments* – how quickly can they be turned into ready money? Some may be almost as good as cash in the bank.

There are three main liquidity ratios. We'll illustrate them by the figures from the two balance sheets for Moneypots Manufacturing shown on pages 82 and 83 – for December 1988 and December 1989:

Current ratio

This is the total of current assets to current liabilities. It's usually given as a ratio rather than a percentage:

current assets		*current liabilities*	
1988 £181 000	:	£79 000	or 2.3 : 1
1989 £194 000	:	£68 000	or 2.8 : 1

This is a very broad indication of the financial health of the business. There's a general feeling that a 2 : 1 ratio is about right, which makes the ratios for Moneypots look very safe – and getting even safer. But remember, a standard like this can only be a guide, not a rule.

Quick assets ratio

This is known as the 'Acid Test' ratio because it is a more stringent measure than the current ratio. It takes into account only those assets that are cash-in-the-bank or the nearest thing to it – debtors and investments that can be quickly cashed (the 'quick assets' of the ratio's name):

quick assets		*current liabilities*	
1988 £181 000	:	£124 000	or 1.6 : 1
1989 £130 000	:	£68 000	or 1.9 : 1

As a rule of thumb, 1 : 1 is generally taken as a safe standard, quick assets more or less in balance with current liabilities. Moneypots Manufacturing looks even better on this measure, and becoming safer still. Too safe perhaps? You may be getting so much safety at the expense of profitability – a point we'll explain in a moment. Again, the standard is a guide not a rule. It depends on the industry and, in a seasonal business, the time of year.

Cash ratio

This ratio, sometimes itself called the 'Liquidity Ratio' is the most rigorous of all. It shows the company's immediate ability to pay its debts, so it omits the debtors. The only assets counted are cash and immediately cashable investments. It's usually given as a percentage:

$$1988 \quad \frac{£17\,000}{£79\,000} \times \frac{100}{1} = 21.5\%$$

$$\frac{Cash}{Current\ liabilities}$$

$$1989 \quad \frac{£13\,000}{£68\,000} \times \frac{100}{1} = 19.1\%$$

There is no general guideline for the cash ratio because so much depends on the nature of the business and the circumstances at the time. Each company has to set its own standard by experience – and anything from 25% to 50% may be considered reasonable as the standard. The

Moneypot ratios look rather tight – and getting tighter. At the end of 1988 the company had just over £21 in the bank to meet each £100 of bills; at the end of 1989, the figure was only £19.

During a period of expansion or when prices are rising, cash is often put under pressure because of heavier expenditures – both capital and revenue – and larger amounts tied up in stock and debtors. In other words the company is running up bigger bills and at the same time getting more money owed to it by customers. The result is often called a 'cash flow problem' or a 'squeeze on liquidity', and the company is forced to borrow more – possibly in short-term loans, possibly in increased overdraft facilities. If the problem can be foreseen, arrangements can be made in advance for the borrowings.

Profitability and liquidity tend to have a negative relationship. What's good for liquidity is often bad for profitability and vice versa. If the various liquidity ratios are high, there may be too much money in current assets earning poor returns. Perhaps there is excess cash that could be invested for better returns inside or outside the business? Perhaps too much money is tied up in stock? Perhaps too little use is being made of supplier credit? Your company is very safe financially speaking, but it's not as profitable as it might be. You have to look at profitability and liquidity ratios *together* to get a reasonable picture of the state of the business.

Actually two of the profitability ratios also tell you something about liquidity. The cost-of-goods-sold/stock ratio indicates how fast stock is moving through the system and so how quickly you can expect it to turn into cash. The sales/debtors ratio shows how fast customers are paying their bills. Both of them give you useful information to help interpret the liquidity ratios.

A study of ratios doesn't solve the problems of your company for you, of course. In fact the ratios don't even tell you what the problems are. *They simply suggest where you should look more closely.* Suppose for instance you notice a persistent fall in the Moneypots Manufacturing sales/debtors ratio from period to period: 600% − 550% − 450% − 400%. Now your debtors are turning over four times a year − your average customer is taking three months' credit instead of two. Your profitability is suffering because too much of your money is in your customers' hands rather than at work in your business. But why is this happening? It could be any one of a number of things − or most likely a combination of them:

- slow invoicing?
- failure to check regularly for overdue accounts?
- failure to send reminders about overdue accounts?
- poor methods of chasing overdue accounts?
- vague or badly judged policies on credit and credit control?
- inadequate staffing in invoicing or credit control sections?
- neglecting to check customers' creditworthiness when opening new accounts?
- not making credit terms clear enough to customers?
- continuing sales to customers whose accounts are overdue?
- failing to involve the sales force in credit control?
- competitors offering better credit terms that your sales force is trying to match?
- worsening trade conditions creating cash-flow problems for customers?

You have to know the cause before deciding action. Simply launching a drive to try to frighten customers into paying may be a poor answer − and may create new and unexpected problems of its own. Once you've found the cause, you can act directly and to the point.

Besides ratios, there's another kind of analysis you can do with the figures to help interpret what's going on in the business. It's given a variety of names: a 'Funds Flow Statement', or a 'Sources and Application of Funds', or let's call it for simplicity:

The 'Funds out of – Funds into' statement

Between one balance sheet and the next, the important question is how the figures have changed – particularly changes that mean the actual movement of cash from one place to another. This is what the 'Funds out of – Funds into' statement is about. It summarises:

1. Funds out of:

From where has money been released inside the business? Has extra money been injected from outside?

Perhaps some fixed assets have been sold. Perhaps some current assets have been reduced – there's less stock, or a smaller amount owed by customers or less money in the bank account. (Yes, those *are* all sources of money.) Perhaps the business has in effect borrowed more by increasing its creditors figure or by owing more to the taxman or anyone else. Very likely there'll be more retained profit in the reserves, and there'll be depreciation too. Most of the sources of extra cash are likely to be internal.

Depreciation of fixed assets? A source of extra cash? That seems a bit hard for those of us who aren't financially orientated to understand. How can those notional amounts of money become real money available for things like new cars or paying the taxes?

For the answer you have to look at what depreciation does to profit, which *is* real money. It reduces it. In the accounts, money is taken out of the profit by depreciation – but actually it's still there in the business. The fact that your office desk is valued now in the accounts at £20 less than it was a year ago doesn't mean that £20 has disappeared. *It's in the profit of the business*. The profit declared has been artificially reduced by £20 to allow for it, but it's still there alongside the profit that has accumulated in the reserves. You simply add it back into the retained profit – which is obviously a source of extra money.

Apart from these internal sources, the business may also have raised money externally – long-term capital. Perhaps a share issue. Perhaps extra borrowed capital. External sources are clearly separated from internal sources in the statement.

2. Funds into:

The extra money put into the assets and into reducing the liabilities. Perhaps further fixed assets have been bought – a property, some equipment, new cars for the sales force. Perhaps stocks have been increased, or the debtors figure, or there's more money in the bank account. Perhaps the amount owing to suppliers has been reduced, or a debt to the taxman paid off. They all require money, the movement of cash into them.

The principle of the 'Funds out of – Funds into' statement is that sources and uses must balance. 'Out of' must equal 'into'! Let's look at a statement drawn up for the two Moneypots Manufacturing balance sheets on pages 82 and 83:

MONEYPOTS MANUFACTURING LIMITED

Funds out of – funds into: 1 January 1989 – 31 December 1989

Funds out of

Internal | £
Extra revenue reserve	2 000
Extra depreciation of fixed assets	14 000
Debenture interest liability	2 000
Reduced cash	4 000
	22 000

External	
Loan capital	25 000
	47 000

Funds into	
Extra fixed assets:	£
office equipment	2 000
sales force cars	15 000
Extra stock	7 000
Extra debtors	10 000
Reduced creditors	5 000
Reduced dividend liability	2 000
Reduced tax liability	6 000
	47 000

Do you see how this works? When you're looking for 'Funds out of' between two balance sheets:
  – on the CAPITAL AND LIABILITIES side, you look for *increases* from the earlier to the later balance sheet – more money from shareholders or from lenders. (This doesn't include increases in *capital* reserves, which are revaluations, not actual cash coming in.)
  – on the ASSETS side, you look for *reductions*. Any reduction among the current assets is more money available. With fixed assets it's in reductions in the *cost*

column. You're looking for money that has come from plant, equipment or property being sold off. (If the cost of something has been written off, that doesn't count.) Increases in the accumulated depreciation also count as extra money, as we've explained.

The search in the balance sheets for 'Funds into' works the other way round:

- on the CAPITAL AND LIABILITIES side, you're looking for *reductions* from the earlier to the later sheet. Less money owing to someone means that cash has been paid out.
- on the ASSETS side, you're looking for *increases* – increases in the current assets, increases in the cost of fixed assets (but *not* any increase that is due to revaluation).

And the sums must balance. 'Into' – where the money has gone – must be the same as 'out of' – where the money has come from.

The point of the exercise is to see whether the changes in the funds make good sense. In the Moneypots example, we've seen that over half the source money comes from a capital loan – which is costing 8% a year. Are the applications likely to produce enough extra profit to pay the £2000-a-year interest *and* maintain the net profitability level? If not, perhaps they're the wrong ways to use the extra funds, and you have more profitable options. Otherwise, if the borrowing is going to reduce profitability and doesn't have any other longer-term advantages, why borrow?

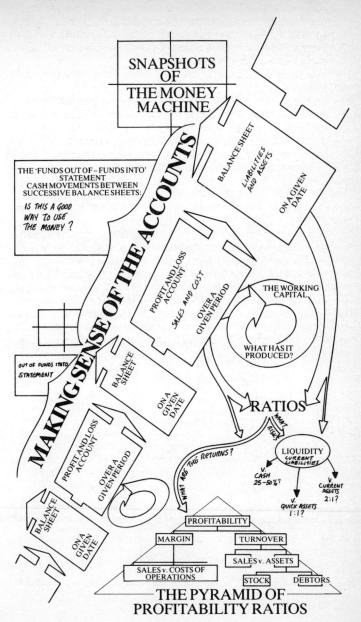

SNAPSHOTS
OF
THE MONEY
MACHINE

THE 'FUNDS OUT OF – FUNDS INTO'
STATEMENT
CASH MOVEMENTS BETWEEN
SUCCESSIVE BALANCE SHEETS:

IS THIS A GOOD
WAY TO USE
THE MONEY ?

BALANCE SHEET

LIABILITIES
AND ASSETS

ON A GIVEN
DATE

MAKING SENSE OF THE ACCOUNTS

PROFIT AND LOSS
ACCOUNT

SALES AND COST

OVER A
GIVEN PERIOD

THE WORKING
CAPITAL

WHAT HAS IT
PRODUCED?

OUT OF FUNDS INTO
STATEMENT

BALANCE
SHEET

ON A
GIVEN
DATE

RATIOS

WHAT
RISKS?

PROFIT AND LOSS
ACCOUNT

OVER A
GIVEN PERIOD

WHAT ARE THE RETURNS?

LIQUIDITY
CURRENT
LIABILITIES

V.
CASH
25–50%?

V.
CURRENT
ASSETS
2:1?

V.
QUICK ASSETS
1:1?

BALANCE
SHEET

ON A
GIVEN
DATE

PROFITABILITY

MARGIN

TURNOVER

SALES v. COSTS OF
OPERATIONS

SALES v. ASSETS

STOCK

DEBTORS

THE PYRAMID OF
PROFITABILITY RATIOS

97

4. Budgets – money plans

As anyone knows, balance sheets and P-and-Ls record what's already happened. After each stage of the game is over, the accountants work out the sums so that everyone knows the score. Shareholders see how their money has been used over the past year. Managers find out that something has gone wrong – when it's too late to stop it. We're accustomed to regarding accounts as the history books of money.

But accounts can be prepared as *plans* too, setting down the scores you intend to reach by the way you'll play the game. This is what budgeting means. Before each period begins, you plan the money: you set up a balance sheet for how you expect the period to begin, and another for the way you intend to make it end. You create a set of budget accounts that explains how you'll get from one to the other. These accounts cover every aspect of the money machine's operations. They describe how the working capital should move and what you intend to spend on fixed assets. They also deal with the money inputs during the period – where the money will come from and how you'll raise any extra capital that's required. In other words, budgeting provides an integrated money plan for the entire business.

Who draws up the plan? Not the accountants! Or not *just* the accountants, we should say. Obviously they're going to be involved, but the money plan has to connect with the operational plan, so both have to be *management's* plans. If a budget is the score a game plan is intended to bring about, the game moves and the scores they produce are all part and parcel of the same design. *A budget is a financial interpretation of an operating plan.* Unless your accountants are going to plan your operations for you, they can't lay sole claim to planning your budget.

Despite this, many managers are pretty cynical about budgets and budgetary control. They can't always be blamed for this. Perhaps they work in organisations where preparation of the budgets is a secretive operation restricted to accountants plus just the top managers – and the things are handed down like tablets of stone from Mount Sinai to the operational managers who are then supposed to make them happen. The exercise is academic if it's divorced from planning the real work of the organisation.

There are many benefits for you as a manager in regularly sitting down with your colleagues and superiors to draw up a budget. *Budgeting makes you think about the future in a clear, systematic way*. You have to visualise the environment in which your business will be operating – how your customers, your market-place and your competition are changing. How busy is the organisation likely to be? What are the economic trends? What is happening to labour and supply sources? How might such things affect your operation? You have to consider the impact of any developments inside the company. Are changes being initiated by managers in other departments or at more senior levels? What are their implications for you? What ideas have you got yourself for your area? Once you've decided what you want to *do*, you've got to convert those future intentions into *figures*. You put your operational plan into a financial form to see whether the things that'll work in physical terms will also work in money terms. The process encourages you to pin down with precision the physical things that you might otherwise leave vague.

There's a wider advantage for the organisation as a whole. The various departments' operational plans have all to be expressed in the same form – money. They're all reduced to a common denominator. *Budgeting provides the machinery for different managers to reconcile their conflicting priorities and to coordinate their plans*. It persuades the managers in a business to pull together as a team, each member agreed on the role he'll play in helping achieve a coherent set of objectives.

Delegation – proper delegation that is – is given a foundation to work on. *Budgetary control reduces the risk of getting delegating confused with dumping*. There's a means to compare performance with plan on the basis of quantified standards, so management can see deviations and take action to correct them. Each manager is more likely to accept his responsibility for economy if he was involved in setting up the financial plan in the first place; the authority he needs for corrective action is more easily defined and handed over to him; and his accountability to his boss can be maintained through regular performance reports.

Apart from encouraging better management, there are also the financial benefits to the organisation. Does the budget provide adequate profitability? Does it avoid liquidity problems? These things can be judged by applying the kinds of analysis we explained in the last chapter – the various ratios and so on – to the budget accounts once they're prepared. And if the figures show the need for extra money at some point, that can be planned for well ahead.

This raises another question: *how far ahead should budgets look*? Discussing the P-and-L in the last chapter, we explained why a year is generally about the right period to get a view of the way the business as a whole is moving – long enough to iron out the seasonal ups and downs of trade. But a year is too long a period for proper management control of its various parts. The plans by which departmental managers operate need mileposts at shorter stages as well as progress checkpoints. And a year is too close a horizon if you're planning major developments in the business as a whole – a new product and the plant to produce it, a big technological change and the equipment to bring it about.

The usual answer is to have an annual budget for the company's operations, but to split it into shorter periods to provide for the more detailed direction and control that is needed within each department – quarterly or even monthly departmental budgets. Over and above these short-run staging posts, there may be a much longer-term plan for major expenditure on fixed assets – looking forward perhaps five, six or seven years or so. This arrangement of periods links in with *the planning time spans of managers*[1] at the various levels – perhaps a month or two for supervisors and other first-line managers, maybe around a year or so for middle-to-senior-level managers, up to several years at the top level. The budget periods for managers at each level can represent realistic timespans for the *operational* plans of managers at that level.

Budgeting

We'll illustrate the way a set of budget accounts might be prepared by turning once again to Moneypots Manufacturing. For the example we'll take your budget for one quarter in the year 1990 – the year following the accounts you saw in the last chapter. You're into the first quarter, so you're already operating on your first budget for the year. You're now budgeting for the *second quarter*, April to June. As a single quarter's budget, it's not an isolated event – more a stage in a journey. It starts from the state the business will have reached by 31 March, and aims to finish the period on 30 June in a state ready to cope with the *following* quarter's business.

[1] discussed in the first book in the series, *What is a Manager?*

MONEYPOTS MANUFACTURING LIMITED
Budgeted balance sheet for 31 March 1990

Capital

	£
Shares:	100 000
Reserves: capital	30 000
Revenue	60 000
Capital loan: 8% debentures	25 000
	215 000

Fixed assets

	Cost or valuation £	Accumulated depreciation £	Net £
Factory property:	60 000	9 000	51 000
Factory plant:	30 000	21 000	9 000
Office equipment:	15 000	5 500	9 500
Salesforce cars:	30 000	15 500	14 500
	135 000	51 000	84 000

Current liabilities

	£
Creditors:	
material suppliers	50 400
plant suppliers	–
Interest:	500
Tax:	14 000
Dividend:	4 000
	68 900

Current assets

	£
Material stocks	30 000
Work-in-progress	7 000
Finished goods	33 000
Total stock:	70 000
Debtors:	98 000
Cash at bank:	31 900
	199 900

Total	£283 900		£283 900

Figure 1

MONEYPOTS MANUFACTURING LIMITED
Budgeted balance sheet for 30 June 1990

Capital		Fixed assets	Cost or valuation	Accumulated depreciation	Net
	£		£	£	£
Shares		Factory property:			
Reserve: capital		Factory plant:			
Revenue		Office equipment:			
Capital loan: 8% debentures	_____	Salesforce Cars:			
	_____				

Current liabilities		Current assets	
	£		£
Creditors:		Material stock	
Material suppliers		Work-in-progress	
Plant suppliers		Finished goods	
Interest:		Total stock:	
Tax:		Debtors:	
Dividend:		Cash at bank:	
	_____		_____
	_____		_____
Total			

Figure 2

The opening balance sheet

The starting point is an estimate of how the balance sheet for 31 March will look (a budget must be prepared some time before its period begins, obviously, so it has to be an estimated balance sheet). Figure 1 shows this opening balance sheet; figure 2 is a prepared form to represent the closing balance sheet – without the figures as yet. We'll ask *you* to fill these in as we work through the budget.

You'll notice some changes between the 31 December 1989 balance sheet on page 79 and the 31 March 1990 balance sheet, suggesting some of the elements in the plans for the first quarter. Debtors are down and suppliers' credit is up:

	31 December	31 March
Debtors	£117 000	£98 000
Creditors	£39 000	£50 400

As we'll find out, sales are increasing, so there must have been quite a tightening on the credit customers are being allowed. More use is being made of suppliers' credit too. Profitability is up – £7 000 after tax for just the first quarter as opposed to £20 000 for the whole of the previous year. There's an extra £3 000 in the Revenue Reserve plus the £4 000 due to be paid as dividend. We'll assume the £18 000 dividend liability in the December 1989 balance sheet has been paid to the shareholders by now. And there's a much healthier cash balance at the bank.

The limiting factor

Your plans are based, like most companies', on the sales figure you think you'll be able to achieve. This is not the only possibility in fact. It's a question of what factor is the most crucial in determining the level of activity the business can achieve during the budget period – the LIMITING FACTOR:
- usually it's the ability to get *sales* that sets the upper limit to the activity level.
- sometimes restrictions in *supplies* are the key. The business can get only limited quantities of an essential raw material or of certain components for assembly or of goods for resale.
- limits to the company's *capacity* may be the crucial factor – which itself may stem from a range of other factors: shortage of people with necessary skills and abilities, limited capacity of machines, even simple lack of physical accommodation.

- a difficulty in obtaining *finance* may be the key restriction on the scale of operation, being itself the cause of some of the foregoing limitations.

The limiting factor is the reference point in a plan – the one thing that everything else has to be geared to. We're taking the most common case by making sales, the ability of the business to penetrate its market, the crucial thing in the Moneypots Manufacturing budget. It's the same in most businesses.

The sales budget

The budgeted sales figure is often called the 'sales forecast'. That suggests it's preordained like the weather, merely a question of guessing the future correctly. It isn't. It's an aim. Its achievement depends on the effectiveness of your sales methods, the organisation of your sales operation, the skill and motivation of your salespeople, the quality of your sales management . . . *It has to be made to happen.* So if low sales are a factor that's severely limiting the business, the real problem may be the way selling is being conducted. True the sales budget has to reflect the general trend of sales and any seasonal pattern in the market. It has to stay within the bounds of probability, otherwise the budget is based on fantasy. But it should also represent a target that will demand the right sort of effort and direction.

The responsibility for the sales budget must rest primarily on the shoulders of sales management. This doesn't deny that marketing in any business ought to be a responsibility shared by all the managers of the business, as we explain elsewhere[1]. But the sales managers and field sales managers are the people to take the lead in defining the targets out in the market place. Among the managers of the business, they stand closest to the market, should have the best idea of how it is moving, and make the operational plans with the most immediate effects on the sales figures. They may look to the accountants for help with data on sales trends analysed by the different product groups, market categories, sales areas, salespeople and so on. They may listen to other managers whose operations have to respond to sales demands. But they have to make the decisions that determine what the target is and how likely it is that it will be achieved.

In Moneypots Manufacturing these decisions are simpler than in most companies because you have just one product – a sales-pack of moneypots you sell for £100. Last year you sold

[1] In another book in the series, *Managing Work*.

7 000 for a sales revenue of £700 000. This year your sales plan is to achieve a sales of 10 000 and a revenue of £1 000 000. Figure 3 shows how that objective is divided between the four quarters, reflecting the seasonal pattern of trade.

	Sales target for 1990		
	Quantity of sales-packs	Selling price £	Revenue £
First quarter	2 200	100	220 000
Second quarter	2 400	100	240 000
Third quarter	2 800	100	280 000
Fourth quarter	2 600	100	260 000

Figure 3

To budget for the second quarter, you need to know the figures for the quarter on either side because one quarter's budget can't be planned in isolation. You have, for instance, to finish the quarter with enough finished goods in stock to set the business up for the peak sales you expect in the third quarter. Over and above the sales requirement in the second quarter, you'll need extra production to lay in the extra stock.

Now it's fairly obvious that the sales activities you plan are going to be a big factor in getting those sales results. In fact, you can hardly make an estimate of sales without looking at the market-place and the competition and deciding what your sales force is going to *do* to get sales. And these sales activities will themselves create costs – which have to be budgeted for. So this is when you draw up a preliminary idea of the sales department's budget. Let's suppose it looks like Figure 4.

Sales department budget 1 April – 30 June 1990	
	£
Sales-force pay and commissions	17 500
Sales office staff pay	6 000
Expenses of travel, entertainment etc	7 000
Car depreciation	1 500
	32 000

Figure 4

Among the figures here is one that you need for the end-of-quarter balance sheet on page 103 – the depreciation of sales-force cars. You've decided not to buy any new cars during the quarter, so the cost figure stays at £30 000. You add a further £1 500 to the accumulated depreciation in the next column, and calculate the net figure for the third column.

The production requirement

From the sales targets defined in the sales budget for the year, you can now plan the finished goods stock during the quarter – which will determine what the factory has to produce. Your policy is to keep enough stock for the next three weeks' sales (one quarter of the total sales for the next period). So you plan to start on 1 April with a stock of 600 of the 2 400 sales-packs for the quarter's sales, and to finish on 30 June with 700 packs in stock for the third quarter's 2 800 target. Figure 5 illustrates this.

Finished goods stock requirements 1 April – 30 June 1990	Quantity of sales-packs
Required for sales	2 400
Required for stock 30 June	700
	3 100
less in stock 1 April	600
Required input to stock	2 500

Figure 5

This gives the basis for all Production's operational plans and budgets. And not only Production. Many different departments will have an interest in finished goods stock, and their interests are quite likely to conflict:
- Sales want enough in stock to cope with any sudden surges in the sales demand. They'll be concerned about their ability to offer customers good service and to avoid delivery delays.
- Production want to maintain a steady, efficient rate of output. They'll be concerned to avoid fluctuations – sudden surges in the demands on Production or slack periods for men and machines.
- The Stock Controller will be concerned about space limitations in his stores. Stock does act as a cushion

between Sales' demands for a flexible response and Production's requirements for steady efficiency. But there will be an upper limit to accommodation, further limited perhaps by the need to keep stock in good condition and to handle it efficiently.
- The Accountant will be concerned with the money trapped in the stock-holding and its effects on profitability and liquidity.
- Product Design may have improved products ready to go into production, which will soon make existing stock obsolete.

The stock budget has to balance all these varying priorities in the best way for the total business. To some extent it is often a compromise between the conflicting interests.

This isn't quite everything in the production requirement. *Work-in-progress* is another factor you have to take into account. Will it increase or reduce during the budget period? Perhaps you're planning an increased utilisation of the production capacity that will create a higher level of work-in-progress; perhaps it's the other way – you're introducing new production techniques that will reduce the level. Either way there's an effect on the production effort that's required, and so on production costs.

We'll assume your opening work-in-progress consisted of 280 units at various stages of production. During the second quarter there'll be a build-up of production for the peak sales you expect in the next quarter, and a corresponding increase in your work-in-progress. You plan to end the quarter with a total of 320 units in progess – 40 more than the starting figure. Since each is on average *half*-finished, you reckon this represents an extra 20 finished units. That's extra production effort that has to be added to the 2500 units to be sent to finished goods stock.

The total production effort required in the quarter is equivalent to an output of 2520 units.

Purchasing and production budgets

We'll suppose you have *STANDARD COSTS* for the materials and the direct labour needed to manufacture each unit – each finished pack of moneypots, that is. The idea is simple in principle, but often complicated to put into practice. It means you have done measurements to establish what each of these two elements *ought* to cost:

- *standard material cost.* A combination of material quantity and price. You've calculated how much material should go into each sales-pack of moneypots, and what should be paid for the required quality of material. This gives you the standard:

standard quantity × *standard price* = *standard material cost*

Your standard material cost is £25 per unit.

- *standard labour cost*. A combination of labour time and pay rates. You've calculated how many hours' labour are needed to produce each sales-pack, and the appropriate rate of pay for the levels of ability and skill that are required:

standard hours × *standard pay rate* = *standard labour cost*

Your standard labour cost is £20 per unit.

Standard costs can make the preparation of budgets far easier, but it's often a long and complicated business to work them out. To calculate a standard labour cost, for instance, you have to analyse all the jobs that labour has to perform in making a product, measure the time required for each one, assess the level of skill and judgement involved and so define the grade of labour and the pay level appropriate for that job. It's a cost-per-unit-of-product approach. In many kinds of business this sort of approach is either inappropriate or unworkable. Another method is to establish the way one thing relates to another – the way material usage relates to sales volumes or revenues, say. Perhaps you find that material costs go up or down by half the amount of rises or falls in sales. If sales increase by 20%, material costs increase by 10%; if sales fall by 10%, material costs drop by 5% ... It's a rule-of-thumb method, rough and ready perhaps, but often accurate enough if you haven't anything better. Even when you do have a more sophisticated method, a simple method like this may provide a useful cross-check.

The material purchases budget will be influenced by your policy for material stock. Let's say you try to keep enough stock for six or seven weeks' production – about one half of the quarter's material usage. You plan to begin the next quarter with 1 200 units of material in stock, and to finish with 1 400 units in stock. From this you calculate your purchases, as shown in Figure 6.

Material purchases budget 1 April – 30 June 1990					
	Quantity		Standard cost £		Total cost £
Required for production	2 520	×	25	=	63 000
Required for material stock 30 June	1 400	×	25	=	35 000
	3 920				98 000
less in stock 1 April	1 200	×	25	=	30 000
Material purchases	2 720				68 000

Figure 6

You now have a value for the material stock you're budgeting for the end-of-quarter balance sheet on page 103.

Like the finished goods stock, your material stock and material purchases budget will be the result of balancing the different and often conflicting interests of different departments:

- Production will want to have a cushion that provides a constant and reliable supply of materials to meet production requirements. They also want a quality that won't create any production problems, or cause complaints from Sales about low-standard merchandise.
- the Materials Stock Controller has his storage capacity to consider, and the needs for efficient materials handling and control.
- the Buyer may wish to keep his costs down by using cheaper sources that cannot provide the reliable quality or delivery that Production and Sales would like. He may want to buy in bulk to take advantage of quantity discounts, but in doing so could create storage problems for the Stock Controller.
- the Accountant is interested in limiting the money tied up in stock. He also has an interest in the credit terms available from the suppliers chosen by the buyer.

The process of planning the budget again focuses everyone's attention on conflicts like these so they can resolve them in the best interests of the business as a whole.

With the production requirements defined, it's now possible to plan the production programme, and calculate the budgets for materials, direct labour and overheads. See the illustration in Figure 7.

```
                       Production budgets
                     1 April – 30 June 1990

MATERIALS BUDGET
Quantity units              Standard cost              Total cost
   2 520          ×             £25          =          £63 000
────────────────────────────────────────────────────────────────
DIRECT LABOUR BUDGET
Quantity units              Standard cost              Total cost
   2 520          ×             £20          =          £50 400
────────────────────────────────────────────────────────────────
OVERHEADS BUDGET                                  £
   Indirect labour                              6 600
   Management salaries                          9 600
   Electricity, gas etc                         2 000
   Plant maintenance                            4 000
   Depreciation of factory property             1 000
   Depreciation of factory plant               2 000
                                               ───────
                                               25 200
                                               ═══════
```

Figure 7

In the closing balance sheet on page 103, enter the figures now
for factory property value. The valuation stays the same at
£60 000; you have £1 000 to add to the accumulated depreciation and a new net value figure to calculate. (Leave the
figures for factory plant for the moment – a capital purchase is
going to change the cost figure there.)

A summary of the three Production budgets enables us to
calculate the total production cost of the finished goods put
into stock and of the extra work-in-progress, and this is illustrated in Figure 8.

```
                    Cost of goods budget
                     1 April – 30 June 1990

                                       £
Materials                           63 000
Labour                              50 400
Overheads                           25 200
TOTAL cost to produce
2 520 units equivalent:             138 600

Budgeted cost per unit:   £138 600  =  £55
                          ───────
                           2 520

Budgeted cost of finished goods
 transferred to stock:       2 500 units at £55 each = £137 500

Budgeted cost of finished goods
 in closing stock:            700 units at £55 each =  £38 500

Budgeted cost of increase in
 work in progress:             20 units equivalent
                                  at £55 each =     1 100
```

Figure 8

This gives you two more figures for the end-of-period balance
sheet on page 103 – the finished goods stock, and the increase
in work-in-progress. We can also draw up the budgeted gross
profit and loss, as shown in Figure 9.

```
                  Gross profit and loss budget
                    1 April – 30 June 1990

                                                         £
        Budgeted sales:                                240 000

        Budgeted cost of finished goods        £
        to stock:                            137 500
plus    Estimated opening stock:              33 000
                                             170 500

less    Budgeted closing stock:               38 500

        Budgeted cost of goods sold:                   132 000
        BUDGETED GROSS PROFIT                          108 000
          (45% of sales)
```

Figure 9

Sales and admin expenses budgets

To arrive at your budgeted net profit, you have to calculate what the selling and admin expenses will be during the period and deduct them from the gross profit figure. We've already seen a budget for the Sales Department (Figure 4). We'll assume a similar budget has been drawn up and agreed for Admin.

The various types of cost have to be estimated in some detail by the managers of the operations the money pays for. Obviously they need to know about the budgets we've been discussing and the operating plans they're based on. They have to gear their calculations of their own variable costs to the planned level of business activity. Sales' budgeted travel expenses have to be geared to the sales activity required to produce the budgeted sales. Admin's clerical wage bill will presumably have some connection with how busy the company is as a whole. Once the budgets are agreed, each manager in these operations will be expected to take responsibility for his part of the budget and the way the actual costs compare with it, so the budgeted costs need to be realistic.

We'll summarise these budgets like this:

Departmental expenses budgets 1 April – 30 June 1990	
	£
Selling expenses	30 500
Depreciation of Sales-force cars	1 500
TOTAL SALES OPERATING COSTS	32 000
Admin expenses	55 800
Depreciation of Office equipment	500
TOTAL ADMIN OPERATING COSTS	56 300

Figure 10

A further figure here for the closing balance sheet – the depreciation of office equipment. You're not planning to buy any further equipment so the cost figure stays at £15 000. Calculate the new figure for accumulated depreciation and the new net value.

The profit and loss budget

This is the *net* profit of course. From the gross profit (figure 9) you have to deduct departmental expenses (figure 10). But that's not all. Don't forget the £25 000 loan you raised last year. Interest has to be paid on it at the rate of 8% a year, 2% a quarter. That's another £500 to be deducted in this quarter's budget.

Once a budget figure for net profit has been calculated, there's a key question: is it adequate? Top management have to look at it in the context of their broad view of the business. Can it provide the investment that's needed in further fixed assets *and* any required growth in working capital *and* a contribution to the dividend that will meet the shareholders' expectations? There's tax to be paid on the profit of course – which is the job of the accountants to calculate, taking account of whatever tax allowances the company can legitimately claim. And on what's left there are decisions to be made about how much to allocate to dividends and how much to retain in the company.

As a guideline, top management may well have set a profitability objective for the year as a whole, to which each of the successive quarterly budgets have to contribute – a target profit margin perhaps, or a required return on assets, or both. If the budgeted profit is too low, perhaps a squeeze on costs somewhere can answer the problem. Perhaps this can't do the trick, and it's back to the drawing board with the entire budgeting exercise. But remember that a single quarter is almost certainly too short a period to make a firm assessment of profitability – you have to take the seasonal pattern into account in deciding what

Profit and loss budget *1 April – 30 June 1990*		
		£
Budgeted gross profit		108 000
less Budgeted Departmental Expenses:	£	
Sales	32 000	
Admin	56 300	
	88 300	
Interest on 8% p.a. debentures	500	
		88 800
Budgeted net profit (8% of Sales)		19 200
less Budgeted tax		7 200
Budgeted net profit after tax		12 000
Revenue reserves on 1 April (estimated)		60 000
		72 000
less Budgeted dividend		5 000
Budgeted revenue reserves on 30 June		67 000

Figure 11

profit target might be set for any particular quarter. We'll assume you've set a target for before-tax profit of 8% of sales for the second quarter. Figure 11 shows the outcome of all the budget calculations and decisions made so far.

Further figures here for the closing balance sheet on page 103. You can add the £500 interest and the £5000 dividend to the appropriate figures in the Current Liabilities (assume you're not making any interest or dividend payments during the quarter). You can also enter the new figure for revenue reserves. But leave the tax figure for the moment – you're going to have to pay off the outstanding tax bill for last year during this quarter, so that will reduce your tax liability quite a bit.

Now we come to a vital part of budgeting – planning the cash. This is the part of the plan that aims to ensure the business stays in business – that it remains solvent.

Cash flow budgets

Although the budget period we're using is a short one – only three months – you can easily go bust within that time if the inflows and outflows of cash don't coincide. So the cash flow budgets need to divide the period into shorter periods to show more exactly *when* the cash movements should happen – at monthly or even shorter intervals. We'll assume that a monthly breakdown is enough to control the cash in Moneypots Manufacturing.

First your **debtors**. The opening balance sheet for the quarter estimates your customers will owe you £98000 on 1 April: how quickly is that likely to be paid off – when should each lump of the money arrive? In addition, your sales budget will add another £240000 of further debts during the quarter. How much of that will be paid off within the quarter and when? What will be outstanding as your debtors figure in the closing balance sheet?

To get answers, you have to estimate two things:

1. *The timing of sales to customers*: how will the sales you've budgeted for be divided between the months in your monthly breakdown? This will have to include the budgeted sales for the first quarter that won't have been paid for by 1 April, as well as the budgeted sales for the second quarter.

You'll remember the full year's sales budget was for a revenue of £220000 in the first quarter and £240000 in the second (figure 3). The monthly figures you estimate as follows:

Sales made in	£
January	80 000
February	70 000
March	70 000
April	70 000
May	80 000
June	90 000

2. *The timing of receipts from customers*: What proportion of customers will pay how quickly? You may regulate this as far as you can through credit policies that your salespeople and credit control staff operate. Perhaps there are features of the payment pattern that you regard as normal for the trade and simply accept and make allowances for – in your pricing perhaps or through discounts. But however the pattern is determined you have to know what it's likely to be if you're going to budget your cash flows. Let's say this is the pattern you expect, reckoned by the value of sales made in each month:

> 10% of sales paid the same month
> 40% of sales paid in the following month
> 50% of sales paid the month after

In other words, 10% of the March sales should be paid for during March; another 40% should be paid during April; and the rest – 50% – should be paid in May.

Putting the two sets of estimates together, the illustration below shows the monthly payments you expect during the quarter:

Budgeted cash receipts from customers 1 April – 30 June 1990								
Sales made in:		Cash receipts in:						
		April		May		June		TOTALS
	£	%	£	%	£	%	£	£
January	80 000		—		—		—	—
February	70 000	50	35 000		—		—	35 000
March	70 000	40	28 000	50	35 000		—	63 000
April	70 000	10	7 000	40	28 000	50	35 000	70 000
May	80 000		—	10	8 000	40	32 000	40 000
June	90 000		—		—	10	9 000	9 000
			70 000		71 000		76 000	217 000

Figure 12

The important figures here are the three at the bottom of the monthly columns for April, May and June – the amount you estimate you should actually collect during each of those months. But the table also tells you some other things. It shows how the debtors figure of £98 000 in the opening balance sheet (figure 1) is made up: £35 000 from sales made in February and £63 000 from March sales (January's sales you reckon should all have been paid for before the quarter begins). It also shows the composition of each month's receipts – the ages and amounts of the debts that are likely to be paid that month.

Another thing can be worked out from the table – the figure for debtors at the end of the quarter, contained in the debtors budget, and shown in Figure 13.

	Debtors budget 1 April – 30 June 1990	£
	Debtors on 1 April	98 000
	Budgeted sales	240 000
		338 000
less	Budgeted cash receipts	217 000
	Budgeted debtors on 30 June	121 000

Figure 13

And this is yet another figure for the closing balance sheet – debtors budgeted at £121 000, an increase of £23 000 from the figure in the opening balance sheet. Why the increase? Because of the increasing sales. If your sales increase and you don't (or can't) do anything to restrict the average length of credit taken by your customers, the result has got to be more working capital tied up in debtors.

Planning these debtor budgets and cash flows – really customer credit control plans of course – ought to be a responsibility of Sales as much as of Accounts. And not only planning them. Just as important is the Sales Department's responsibility for operating to them. Sales managers often claim that credit control has nothing to do with the Sales Department, but can they really turn their backs on the problem – when for instance their salesman continue selling to customers who are on the credit control Stop List? And that really does happen. Or what about the problem discussed in another book in the series, *Managing Work*, in a section about pricing and credit control in marketing:

". . . look at the way the company chases up the late payers among its customers. Often a company will leave this vital work to its credit control clerks. But they aren't usually equipped with the people-skills to persuade the customer to pay up without risking the loss of his future business. Remember the point of the organisation's purpose – 'to create customers' – is that the organisation *keeps* them as customers. It can neither afford to give extended free loans because its clerks aren't persuasive enough, nor to lose a customer simply because of an offensive letter or telephone call.

"The answer is not to leave it to the credit control clerks. It's a job that demands the special skills of the salesman. And don't go saying 'but our salesmen are there to *sell*, not to act as debt-collectors.' Selling includes seeing that the money comes in, otherwise your sales force is acting as Father Christmas to your customers. Of course, a lot can be done with a series of good chasing letters (but *good* chasing letters, not the kind of distant, formal or threatening missives so many organisations seem to use). If they don't do the trick, it's the salesman's job to go in there and charm the customers into paying. *He* has the skills – *and* the relationship with each customer – to do it."

Next your **creditors**. Future payments to your materials suppliers can be analysed in much the same way as the debtors' cash flow. The same two factors apply – the timings of your purchases and the timings of your payments – and you'll have to use the same monthly time-periods to make the timings of cash inflows and outflows connect. These are your estimates:

1. *The timing of purchases from suppliers.* The budgeted material purchases for the second quarter are £68 000 (figure 6), and we'll assume the budgeted figure for the first quarter is £63 000. The monthly breakdown is:

Purchases made in:	£
January	21 000
February	21 000
March	21 000
April	22 000
May	23 000
June	23 000

2. *The timing of payments to suppliers.* This is the pattern, planned jointly by the Buyer and the Accountants:

  0% of purchases paid the same month
20% of purchases paid the next month
20% of purchases paid the month after that
60% of purchases paid the month after that again.

This means that of the purchases in March, say, none will be paid that month; 20% should be paid during April; another 20% should be paid in May; and 60% should be paid in June.

The two sets of factors will produce these budgeted monthly payments during the quarters, as shown in the illustration below.

		Budgeted cash payments to suppliers 1 April – 30 June 1990						
Purchases made in:		Cash payments in:						TOTALS
		April		May		June		
	£	%	£	%	£	%	£	£
January	21 000	60	12 600		—		—	12 600
February	21 000	20	4 200	60	12 600		—	16 800
March	21 000	20	4 200	20	4 200	60	12 600	21 000
April	22 000		—	20	4 400	20	4 400	8 800
May	23 000		—		—	20	4 600	4 600
June	23 000		—		—		—	—
			21 000		21 200		21 600	63 800

Figure 14

119

Again, it's the figures at the bottom of the monthly column that are the important ones. You also see the make-up of the £50 400 for suppliers' credit in the opening balance sheet (figure 1) – that's the sum of the totals for January, February and March to be paid during the second quarter. And you can calculate from the figures in this table the creditors' budget for that end of the quarter:

Creditors budget (Material Suppliers) 1 April – 30 June 1990	
	£
Creditors on 1 April	50 400
Budgeted purchases	68 000
	118 400
less Budgeted cash payments	63 800
Budgeted creditors on 30 June	54 600

Figure 15

You can enter into the closing balance sheet the budgeted creditors figure for material suppliers.

Cash receipts from customers and payments to suppliers of materials don't complete the picture of cash movements. True, in the example we're using, customers' payments are the only income there is – we're assuming the company has no investments and so no income from that source. But there will be many more cash outflows than the ones to the suppliers of your production materials. Wage and salary payments for one thing, payments for things like office supplies, electricity and telephones for another – the cash payments included in Production overheads and the Departmental expenses budgets. As well as calculating the total costs for the quarter, managers and accountants will have to estimate the month-by-month timing of all these payments before they can complete the cash flow budgeting.

Besides regular payments like these, we'll assume there will be two major cash outflows during the quarter:

1. The tax bill for the previous year (recorded in the 31 December 1989 balance sheet) – £8 000 out of the £14 000 tax liability budgeted in the opening balance sheet for the second quarter. This will be paid in April. The other £6 000 of the total sum will remain as a liability, plus the £7 200 tax liability budgeted on the second quarter's profit (figure 11). You can now enter this tax liability in the closing balance sheet on page 103.

2. Part-payment for the purchase of some new plant for the factory. Much of the existing plant is old and out-dated – as the large amount of accumulated depreciation on it might suggest. Over the next year or so, a programme to re-equip the factory has been planned, of which this is the first step. £20 000-worth of new equipment will be installed during the quarter. Half the cost will be paid to the plant suppliers during June, and the other half will become a further liability among creditors in the closing balance sheet.

In the closing balance sheet, you can add £20 000 to the Factory Plant cost under Fixed Assets. The depreciation figure on factory plant remains as budgeted in the Production Overheads Budget (figure 7), so you can now calculate the accumulated depreciation figure and the new net value for plant. This completes the fixed assets part of the balance sheet, and you can calculate the totals here.

The £10 000 liability that will be owed to the plant suppliers at the quarter's end has to be entered under creditors. You should now find that the figures for current liabilities are also complete; again, calculate the total of current liabilities.

Apart from the new figure you've already entered for revenue reserves, there will be no changes to the amounts of capital between the opening and closing balance sheets. Shares, capital reserves and capital loan will all stay at the same values, so you can transfer these figures to the closing balance sheet, and calculate the total capital figure.

Just one figure is now missing. What will be the budgeted cash at bank in the closing balance sheet? That is the figure you calculate in the cash budget, as illustrated in Figure 16.

```
                        Cash budget
                      1 April – 30 June

                                    £                £
Budgeted Cash at bank, 1 April              31 900 (from fig. 1)

Budgeted cash receipts from customers      217 000 (from fig. 12)

Total cash available                       248 900

Budgeted cash payments:

  to materials suppliers          63 800 (from fig 14)
  production direct labour        50 400 (from fig. 7)
  production overhead expenses    22 200 (from fig. 7)
  selling expenses                30 500 (from fig. 10)
  admin. expenses                 55 800 (from fig. 10)
  tax                              8 000
  to plant supplier               10 000  (see pages 119–120)

Total cash payments                        240 700
Budgeted cash at bank, 30 June               8 200
```

Figure 16

Enter £8 200 as cash at bank in the closing balance sheet
and calculate the total for current assets. Add that to the total
net value for fixed assets above and put the sum total of assets
at the bottom on the right-hand side. Add the totals of capital
and current liabilities and put that sum total at the bottom on
the left. The two sum totals should be the same figure: where
the money is *from* must equal what the money is *in*.

One point might possibly puzzle you about the expenses
figures in the cash budget. *They all exclude depreciation.*
That's because depreciation isn't an actual cash payment – as
we're assuming all the rest of the expenses are in each case.
We're also assuming these expenses will be paid in full during
the second quarter (if any of them weren't actually going to be
paid before the quarter's end, they would have to be added to
the creditors figures in the closing balance sheet, of course).

Finally the cash budget can be analysed into a
month-by-month cash flow to see how the cash fluctuates
during the quarter. On the face of it, the bank balance will stay
in credit – but is that really so? You can't be sure without doing
a cash flow budget. In the cash flow that follows, we've
assumed the way the departmental expenses given in the cash
budget will be phased month by month as the tempo of
activity builds up through the quarter. See Figure 17.

The 'closing cash' figures are the ones to look at here. As it
happens, they are positive throughout. If there had been a
temporary move into deficit in one of the months, it would

have been worth knowing so that an overdraft could be arranged with the bank – or perhaps some payment delayed for a few weeks. But the fall in the cash balance from the start to the end of the period as a whole would need to be considered. A drop from £31 900 to £8 200 is a big one.

	April £	May £	June £
Budgeted cash flow 1 April – 30 June 1990			
Opening cash	31 900	21 900	18 900
Budgeted cash receipts	70 000	71 000	76 000
Cash available	101 900	92 900	94 900
Budgeted cash payments:			
to materials suppliers	21 000	21 200	21 600
production labour	16 000	16 800	17 600
production overheads	7 000	7 400	7 800
selling expenses	10 000	10 000	10 500
admin expenses	18 000	18 600	19 200
to plant supplier			10 000
tax	8 000		
Cash outflow	80 000	74 000	86 700
Closing cash	21 900	18 900	8 200

Figure 17

Assessing the budget

With the opening and closing balance sheets and the sales and profit figures in the budget accounts, you can now calculate the ratios we illustrated in the previous chapter.

Profitability

The *profit margin* ratio of the quarter's budget has already been given (figure 11). But what is the *return on total assets*? Calculate this yourself using the total asset figure you worked out in the closing balance sheet:

$$\frac{\text{profit}}{\text{assets}} = \frac{£19\,200}{£} \times \frac{100}{1} = \qquad \%$$

Figure 18

Remember, this percentage is the return for one quarter. To find the equivalent return for a full year, multiply the percentage by 4. Of course, from the figures for only three months, you're unlikely to get a result that's valid over longer periods. But it may still be valid to compare the ratio for this quarter with the ratio for the same quarter last year and the year before – or with the ratios for other companies in the trade for the same period.

Liquidity

Given the three liquidity ratios for the opening balance sheet, try calculating them for the closing balance sheet to see in which direction they are moving:

Current ratio	Current assets	:	Current liabilities	
1 April	£199 900	:	£68 900	= 2.9 : 1
30 June	£	:	£	= : 1

Figure 19

Quick assets ratio	Quick assets		Current liabilities	
1 April	£129 900	:	£68 900	= 1.9 : 1
30 June	£	:	£	= : 1

Figure 20

Cash ratio

$$\frac{\text{cash}}{\text{current liabilities}} \qquad \text{1 April} \quad \frac{£31,900}{£68,900} \times \frac{100}{1} \quad = 46.3\%$$

$$\text{30 June} \quad \frac{£}{£} \times \frac{100}{1} \quad = \qquad \%$$

Figure 21

The first two ratios for 1 April are very high – there would be no harm in a lower ratio in each case at the quarter's end. The cash ratio for 1 April will be a big improvement on the ratio we calculated from the 31 December 1989 balance sheet (19.1%). But what will it be on 30 June? How do you interpret the ratios you get from the closing balance sheet?

You can also prepare a 'Funds out of – Funds into' statement as illustrated below. In this case, we'll ask you to write in the sources and the uses of the funds as well as calculating the figures.

Funds out of – Funds into: 1 April-30 June 1990

Funds out of   £
    internal sources : _____   _____
    _____   _____

    _____   _____
    external sources : _____   _____
Funds into   £
    _____   _____
    _____   _____
    _____   _____

If you now want to check your own figures in all the exercises we've asked you to complete here, you'll find the correct answers on pages 205–207.

Perhaps the way we've described a budget being built up suggests it's a very straightforward process, following a fixed sequence of steps that neatly slot into one another as the plan develops. Don't be misled! It's never as smooth as that. Maybe there does have to be a reference point – a limiting factor that everything else depends on, like the sales figures on which the Moneypots budgets were based. But a lot of the budget-planning activities go on concurrently. In the early stages managers sketch their preliminary ideas for themselves, perhaps before they have any finalised figures about the activity level to assume. As the plans take shape, there's a great deal of conferring and adjustments of the initial figures to be made before the budget settles into its final form. Sometimes the entire plan has to be reconstructed because of a late change in a vital figure.

One thing alone can be certain. The actual events will never turn out exactly as the budget indicated. But that is the point of having a budget for managers to use as a control for events as they actually happen.

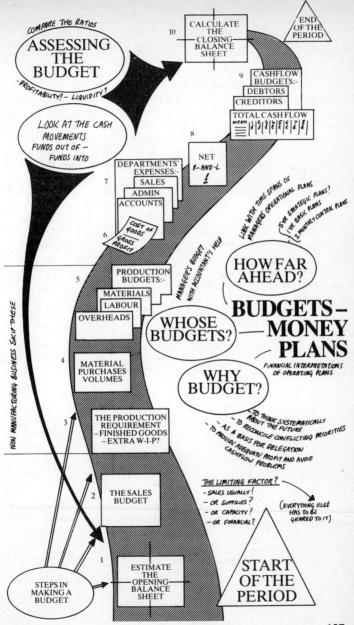

COMPARE THE RATIOS

ASSESSING THE BUDGET

- PROFITABILITY? - LIQUIDITY?

LOOK AT THE CASH MOVEMENTS FUNDS OUT OF — FUNDS INTO

END OF THE PERIOD

10 CALCULATE THE CLOSING BALANCE SHEET

9 CASHFLOW BUDGETS:-
DEBTORS
CREDITORS
TOTAL CASH FLOW
WEEK

8 NET P- AND -L

7 DEPARTMENTS' EXPENSES:-
SALES
ADMIN
ACCOUNTS

COST OF GOODS

6 GROSS PROFIT

LINK WITH TIME SPANS OF MANAGERS OPERATIONAL PLANS
5YR STRATEGIC PLANS?
1YR BASIC PLANS
3 MONTHLY CONTROL PLANS

MANAGER'S BUDGET WITH ACCOUNTANT'S HELP

5 PRODUCTION BUDGETS:-
MATERIALS
LABOUR
OVERHEADS

HOW FAR AHEAD?

WHOSE BUDGETS?

BUDGETS — MONEY PLANS

FINANCIAL INTERPRETATIONS OF OPERATING PLANS

WHY BUDGET?

4 MATERIAL PURCHASES VOLUMES

3 THE PRODUCTION REQUIREMENT — FINISHED GOODS — EXTRA W-I-P?

- TO THINK SYSTEMATICALLY ABOUT THE FUTURE
- TO RECONCILE CONFLICTING PRIORITIES
- AS A BASIS FOR DELEGATION
- TO PROVIDE ADEQUATE PROFIT AND AVOID CASHFLOW PROBLEMS

NON MANUFACTURING BUSINESS SKIP THESE

THE LIMITING FACTOR?
- SALES USUALLY!
- OR SUPPLIES?
- OR CAPACITY?
- OR FINANCIAL?

(EVERYTHING ELSE HAS TO BE GEARED TO IT)

2 THE SALES BUDGET

1 ESTIMATE THE OPENING BALANCE SHEET

STEPS IN MAKING A BUDGET

START OF THE PERIOD

5. Budgetary control

The point of budgeting is to give managers the means to control the money involved in their operations through their control of the physical activities. For that to happen, the division between the various budget accounts of the things the figures stand for has to match the actual division of responsibilities among the managers and the authority they've been given to deal with problems in their areas. Unless each manager is clear about which figures he is responsible for – and which not – you can hardly expect effective management action when gaps appear between budget and actual performance. What's more, it has to be clear which figures are controllable by the managers involved, which figures they can be said to influence if not actually control, and which figures are totally beyond their sway.

Ideally, managers' responsibilities and the extent of their authority are defined in job descriptions. In practice most job descriptions are quite useless for seeing how *financial* responsibilities are divided.[1] They are often too vague and generalised, are frequently out of date, and are non-existent in many organisations. Structure diagrams of the organisation are irrelevant because they aren't designed to show how responsibilities are allocated – simply the lines of formal communication.

In Moneypots Manufacturing you are of course using a sensible system of budgetary control, so you've probably already defined the financial responsibilities and authority of your managers. In fact you must have done this because they were involved in preparing the budget, which they could hardly be if they weren't aware of which costs and activities each one was to look after.

The divisions between the different departmental budgets also showed you had done some classification of your accounting headings so that each cost can be properly allocated to the department and manager responsible. This is the basis of the company's **accounts code** which gives you a label (reference letters or figures) for each bit of paperwork

---

[1] Another book in the series, *Managing Work*, discusses a form of job description which is helpful.

that enters the accounting system. This helps Accounts to prevent any money from being double-entered into the system or from being left out altogether.

The reporting system by which summaries of all these figures reach managers is a vital part of the whole budgetary system. Budgetary control requires reports from accountants to managers. The accountants are busily collecting all the raw figures from the operations and recording them in their ledgers. The managers don't want that mass of detailed figurework, but they do want to know where the figurework says they are in relation to where the budget says they ought to be. That's the job of the reports – to enable managers to spot the differences (**variances** the accountants call them) between budgeted figures and actual figures so they can investigate and decide what to do.

The accountants are responsible for providing these reports. But don't let them kid you they alone decide the kinds of information that go into them. You and your managerial colleagues need to have a say, for many reasons:
- you know better than the accountants what goes on in your department. So you ought to know what sort of information is useful to you and what isn't.
- you know the strengths and weaknesses of the system and of your subordinates, so you know what needs watching.
- you're getting operational information already. To understand what's pushing the cost one way or another, you've got to be able to link the figures in the reports from the accountants to that operational information. Unless you get the right figures, that's impossible.
- you know the sorts of things that can go wrong, how serious their effects can be elsewhere in the system, how quickly it's possible to spot something going off the rails. So you know which is the really vital control information, and which is useful but not essential.
- you know how quickly you want information. You know when it's worth giving up something in detail or accuracy for the sake of fast news.

If you don't get a share in the decisions about the form and timing of the reports, it'll be no surprise if you fail to get the information you actually need. You have to get stuck in there with the accountants to define what figures the reports should contain, how they are to be laid out so that you make easy sense of them, how frequently they should be produced, how quickly after the end of each reporting period ... If you're going to use budgetary control, you've got to get the right kinds of figures at the right level of detail at the right time — right, that is, for you not for the accountants.

All the same, you've got to be sensible. There can't be a completely tailor-made job done for every manager in the outfit. The reports the accountants produce must be standardised to a large extent, simply to keep down the costs of accounting. Demands for a lot of ad hoc reports make for inefficient accounting. They may affect the quality and accuracy of the *standard* reports because of overloading the Accounts staff and reducing their interest in trying to do a good job.

If you want something in your department's reports that isn't needed by anyone else and that will cost something to provide, does the benefit to you justify the cost to the Accounts Department? That's a difficult question to answer: the accountants won't be able to give a precise cost, and you'll find it hard to quantify an intangible benefit. But it's an essential question to ask, and not only of one-off ad hoc requests either. It should be regularly asked of all the budgetary reports that are produced by the system: "do we get best value out of the money and effort they're costing the Accounts Department?" "Could any changes in them improve the quality of the management decisions enough to make the costs of the changes worth paying?"

The purpose of the reporting system is to give managers a regular **measurement of performance**. At different management levels and in different departments, the yardsticks will be different, of course:

- at top management level, the total profitability of the business is the most likely criterion — the *margin* or more likely the *return on assets* ratio, perhaps both.
- the manager heading up a branch or independent unit (a shop or hotel in a chain for instance) may measure his performance in the same way. He is running a 'profit centre' — in effect a business on its own.
- the manager of a sales department or a sales team is probably judged on *actual sales to budgeted sales*, or on *growth in sales* (if budgets don't exist). Sometimes it's fairer to relate results and costs — a *sales revenue/selling costs* ratio.
- managers in other departments directly involved in providing the 'product' (i.e. those in Line as opposed to Staff functions) are quite likely to use a *cost-per-unit-of-product* as the measure, if that is possible.
- managers of Staff or service functions can sometimes use

131

an *artificial 'profit' measure* where the accounting system includes a method of transfer pricing – one department 'selling' its services to another at cost plus a suitable mark-up. But beware: this can have its problems if the service is one the 'customer' departments find they can buy cheaper outside.

The commonest yardsticks of all are those the budget itself defines – the budgeted costs – and perfectly valid yardsticks they are as long as the budget is itself a realistic but also challenging target. Managers measure *how closely their actual costs match the budgeted costs* for their areas. If the target is a challenging one, it often won't be matched. There are bound to be differences between budgeted and actual figures, the 'variances' of budgetary control reports.

Variances

Variances – their measurement and interpretation – are the basis of budgetary control. As a manager you're interested in three things:

1. What variances exist? In what particular cost factors?
2. In which direction does the variance lie – good or bad? Is it a favourable or adverse variance?
3. How big is the variance? Is it really significant?

The questions focus attention on the particular aspects of a department's operations – or of the entire business – that need attention. They reveal the problems so that causes can be investigated. They pinpoint the factors that are controllable by particular managers. They show what is working well so that lessons can be learned and applied elsewhere.

This is all very well, but there's one major problem in the way a budget is constructed. *It's based on an assumed level of activity.* For the Moneypots budget, it was all determined by the sales target. Everything else in the budget – the production overheads, the sales and admin Expenses – they all started from the assumption that the business would be selling 240 000 sales-packs of moneypots during the three months. *What if that doesn't happen?* If you were to sell 250 000 sales-packs, would you still expect each department's expenses to match the figures you originally budgeted? What if sales actually come to only 230 000 sales-packs? What expenses would be reasonable to expect then? Obviously there would be variances between budgeted and actual figures, but would they be significant?

The problem isn't so much with the direct costs of materials and labour – not for the goods you actually make, anyway. You've got standard costs for those, so it's not difficult to recalculate the figures for a different volume of production. Nor is there much difficulty with fixed costs that are unaffected by the change – things like depreciation costs, management and staff salaries in Sales and Admin., property rent and rates, insurance premiums (if those were among your costs). The real problem is with overheads that do vary to some extent with changes in activity level: overtime payments, electricity and power supplies, telephone charges, consumable stores, plant maintenance and repair work . . .

For these you need to know *how costs behave when levels of activity change*:

- which costs don't vary for the size of change you've actually got? Given a big enough change in activity level, almost any cost will vary – 'fixed' costs are fixed only over a certain range of different levels of activity. So you have to find out which costs are fixed *for the actual size of change you're looking at*.
- for the costs that vary, *at what rate do they vary*? How do you establish the new cost level for a new activity level?

The point of knowing this is to calculate the kind of adjustment you have to make to your original budget to get a valid comparison with actual performance.

If your budget doesn't make any allowance for actual activity levels being different from those budgeted, it's called a *FIXED BUDGET*. If it does allow for variations, there's more than one way to do it. One is to calculate a range of different budget settings – what is known as a *FLEXIBLE BUDGET*. Suppose one had been prepared for the Production Overheads budget on page 110. It might have calculated the costs for the quarter's production volumes ranging from 2400 to 2600 units in steps of 50, like the illustration below.

Production overheads: flexible budget 1 April – 30 June 1990					
	Production quantity:				
	2400	2450	2500	2550	2600
Overhead cost items:	£	£	£	£	£
Indirect labour	6070	6420	6550	6780	7110
Management salaries	9600	9600	9600	9600	10400
Electricity, gas etc.	1840	1910	1980	2050	2120
Plant maintenance	3500	3500	4000	4000	4500
Depreciation:					
factory property	1000	1000	1000	1000	1000
factory plant	2000	2000	2000	2000	2000
	24010	24430	25130	25430	27130

In this example, some costs vary with production volume – though not always in exact proportion. Electricity and gas *are* in proportion, indirect labour only roughly so (we're assuming very precise calculations for each level of activity). Other costs are unchanged over a number of steps, then jump to a new level. Yet others stay the same over the full production range covered – depreciation in this case.

Another possibility is the *VARIABLE BUDGET*. You accept the budget cannot be fixed. But rather than attempting to work out in advance a series of precise costings for different production volumes, you prefer to adjust the budget by a standard rate. You might say here for instance that overheads are roughly £10 per unit of production. That wouldn't give you so exact a costing for any particular level of production in the 2400–2600 unit range, but it might be near enough.

Let's illustrate how a variable budget works with a simple example. Suppose you're budgeting for the costs of running your car during the coming year. Your budget includes regular servicing at your local garage, and petrol costs:

- servicing you reckon will cost a 'fixed' figure of £400 for the year.
- petrol you estimate on the car's mpg and the current price of petrol. You reckon you'll travel 20 000 miles at a cost of 5p per mile – so your budgeted figure for petrol is £1000.

At the end of the year you add up your actual spending and compare it with the budget:

Car costs for the year: fixed budget			
	Budget £	Actual £	Variance £
Servicing	400	350	50 favourable
Petrol	1000	1400	(400) adverse

On the face of it you've performed well on servicing costs and badly on petrol costs. But it's not as simple as that. Actually you covered 30 000 miles, so you've got to adjust the budget to fit. At 5p a mile your petrol costs should have been £1500:

Car costs for the year: variable budget			
	Adjusted budget £	Actual £	Variance £
Servicing	400	350	50 favourable
Petrol	1500	1400	100 favourable

There was actually a bigger favourable variance on petrol than there was on servicing.

You might do some further investigation to find out why. Was it the result of economical driving, or of finding a cheaper source of petrol? It must be one or the other and it would perhaps be worth knowing which. In fact they illustrate the two main factors in any variances:

- *volume*: economy in the *use* of whatever is being considered, whether it's material quantity or labour time or accommodation space . . . Here it would be low petrol consumption because of economical driving.
- *price*: the unit cost of the material or labour time or accommodation space or whatever – how much it cost to *buy*. Here it would be finding a cheaper petrol source.

Both factors could be adverse. Both could be favourable. Or one could be adverse while the other is favourable. You might actually have used more petrol than the volume budgeted, but have found so cheap a supply that it more than compensated for the extra petrol you used.

The servicing cost variance raises the same questions. Did you manage to find a cheaper garage to do the servicing (a price variance)? Or did you have fewer services done to save the money (a volume variance)? If so, was it wise to reduce the amount of servicing when mileage was actually a good deal more than budgeted? Could it be false economy? Anyway, servicing probably shouldn't be regarded as a fixed cost, but as another variable or a semi-variable cost which depends at least partly on mileage.

To apply this to the workings of a business organisation – Moneypots Manufacturing for instance – there are three basic cost elements in which you might find variances, and one revenue element:

- *the costs of materials*
- *the costs of direct labour*
- *the costs of overheads*
- *the revenue from sales*

How do you interpret variances in them? Let's take each in turn.

Material cost variances

We're assuming you have a standard cost for each of the materials you use to make one of your products – a sales-pack of moneypots. There's the moneyclay used for the pots (very expensive!), the paints to decorate them, the board for the sales-packs and so on. Each standard cost is made up of the same two elements:

standard quantity × standard price = standard material cost

For instance, you've calculated exactly how much moneyclay is needed for each completed sales-pack, and a price that ought to be paid for the quality you need. Suppose the figures looked like this:

standard quantity	standard price	standard cost
10 kgs per sales-pack	× £1.50 per kg	= £15 per sales-pack

At that £15-per-unit standard cost, the total budgeted cost for the clay for the 2520 products to be manufactured in the April – June quarter is £37 800. You get to the end of the quarter and add up the actual cost to find it's £45 150 – an adverse variance of £7 350 apparently. Why has this happened?

First you look at the *actual* number of sales-packs manufactured. No point in trying to analyse the variance before you've adjusted the budget to the real level of activity. We'll suppose the production figure was actually 2580:

adjusted budget
2580 × £15 = £38 700

The adverse variance was actually £6 450, which isn't *quite* so bad. But what caused it?

A usage variance is one possibility. The factory used more than the standard 10 kg per set of pots – which would have added up to a total of 25 800 kg. for the output in the adjusted budget, as in the following illustration.

Material costs: variance report no 1					
	usage		price		cost
Budget:	25 800 kg	×	£1.50 per kg	=	£38 700
Actual:	30 100 kg	×	£1.50 per kg	=	£45 150
Variance:	(4 300 kg)		——		(£6450)
	adverse				adverse

This would point your investigation towards Production and what was going on inside the factory. Were they putting too much material into the pots? Was it being wasted through inefficiency or carelessness? And what caused *that* problem in turn? Bad production techniques? Inadequate production planning and control? Poor training of the workforce? Lax supervision? Low morale? Perhaps the quality of the materials obtained by Buying was at fault – causing wastage and rejection of goods in production. It's even possible that the standard is too tight and needs changing to make it more realistic . . .

A price variance is another possibility:

Material costs: variance report no 2					
	usage		*price*		*cost*
Budget:	25 800 kg	×	£1.50 per kg	=	£38 700
Actual:	25 800 kg	×	£1.75 per kg	=	£45 150
Variance:	———		(25p per kg) adverse		(£6450) adverse

The buyer paid more than the standard price per kilogram. This would suggest looking into the purchasing operation. Were negotiations with suppliers to blame – being too ready to accept price increases, not energetic enough in looking for ways to hold down the price per kg? Was there an attempt to reduce the money invested in stock by buying in smaller – and more expensive – consignments? Or has a general and unavoidable rise in prices made the existing standard no longer a practicable proposition?

Joint variances in both factors are the most likely. Perhaps both have moved in the same direction – as adverse variances, say:

Material costs: variance report no 3					
	usage		*price*		*cost*
Budget:	25 800 kg	×	£1.50 per kg	=	£38 700
Actual:	26 250 kg	×	£1.72 per kg	=	£45 150
Variance:	(450 kg) adverse		(0.22p per kg) adverse		(£6450) adverse

... in which case there's a small problem in calculating how much of the total £6450 adverse variance is due to Production's usage, and how much to Buying's price. The problem is how to avoid saddling either department with the costs of the other department's variance. To achieve this:

– Production's usage variance is costed at the budgeted price per kg, not the actual price paid by Buying:

(450 kg) adverse × £1.50 per kg = (£675) adverse

– Buying's price variance is costed at the budgeted usage figure, not the actual usage in Production:

(22p per kg) adverse = 25 800 kg = (£5676) adverse

This shows quite clearly that more of the problem is in the price variance, so if there's any question of where the priority is for investigation, this calculation has answered it.

There is a tiny further problem, one that possibly bothers the accountants more than the manager. There's a missing £99 in the combined variances:

	£
Production's usage variance	(675) adverse
Buying's price variance	(5676) adverse
	(6351) adverse

. . . But that figure doesn't tally with the real total variance of £6450. Why the missing £99? Because splitting the two departments' variances has left out the bit of variance that's the *combination of usage and price variances*, that's why:

(450 kg) usage variance × (22p per kg) price variance = (£99)

To tidy away this loose end, many accountants would tack it on to the price variance – and Buying would then have the responsibility for £5775 of adverse variance in total. But this is just an accountancy wriggle. The real responsibility for the odd £99 should rightly be shared between the two departments.

There would be a similar problem if both variances were favourable. Who gets the credit for the bit of the total saving that is due to *both* departments? Does it really matter?

Variances in the two factors can also go in opposite directions, of course. An adverse variance in one factor can be offset or partly offset by a favourable variance in the other. Suppose the variance analysis had shown this:

Material costs: variance report no 4			
	usage	*price*	*cost*
Budget:	25 800 kg	× £1.50 per kg	= £38 700
Actual:	30 000 kg	× £1.29 per kg	= £38 700
Variance:	(4 200 kg) adverse	£0.21 per kg favourable	——

Now the total cost variance is nil. Yet there are quite big variances in the two factors that cancel each other out:

- Production's usage variance is costed at the budgeted price. They can't claim the credit for the price the Buying Department has actually paid:

(4 200 kg) adverse × £1.50 per kg = (£6 300) adverse

- Buying's price variance is now costed at the *actual* usage. This assumes they can claim the credit for offsetting the financial effects of Production's excess usage:

  21p per kg favourable × 30 000 kg = £6 300 favourable.

So this time the sums do add up:

	£
Production's usage variance	(6 300) adverse
Buying's price variance	6 300 favourable
	—

Production is asked to investigate the large excess in usage, while Buying is congratulated on their success in reducing the price. Only later is it found that the cheaper material created manufacturing problems in Production – hence the adverse usage variance – and many quality complaints received by Sales from customers. So was that favourable price variance really doing the business a favour?

Labour cost variances

The standard labour cost is for *direct* labour of course. Indirect labour will be a part of your overheads. The standard is made up in much the same way as your standard cost for materials – with a volume element (the volumes of time required) and a

139

price element (the appropriate pay rates for the required grades of labour). We'll assume you've done these calculations for each kind of operation involved in making your moneypots – moulding, painting, oven-firing and so on:

standard hours × standard pay rate = standard labour cost

For one of your operations – the moulding operation, say – you've got these figures per product:

standard hours		standard pay rate		standard labour cost
2 hrs	×	£3 per hr	=	£6

At this standard, the budgeted cost of moulding the 2580 sets of pots actually made in the quarter is £15 480. The variances you might get in the actual figures work in much the same ways as the material variances – just with different names:

An efficiency variance is a volume difference – a variance between standard and actual hours, when the employees have taken on average a shorter or longer time than standard for the number of products made:

Labour costs: variance report no 1				
	hours		rate	cost
Budget:	5 160	× £3 per hr		= £15 480
Actual:	4 840	× £3 per hr		= £14 520
Variance:	320 hrs favourable	——		£ 960 favourable

A rate variance is a price difference – a variance in the wage rate actually paid to the employees:

Labour costs: variance report no 2				
	hours		rate	cost
Budget:	5 160	× £3 per hr		= £15 480
Actual:	5 160	× £3.25 per hr		= £16 770
Variance:	——	(£0.25 per hr) adverse		(£ 1 290) adverse

Joint variances are again the norm – it would be very unusual to find a variance in one of the two factors and none at all in the other. The analysis of the variances to separate the effects of labour efficiency and pay rate can be very revealing for the managers responsible for the people, as shown in the illustration below.

Labour costs: variance report no 3					
	hours		*rate*		*cost*
Budget:	5 160	×	£3 per hr	=	£15 480
Actual:	4 840	×	£3.25 per hr	=	£15 730
Variances:	320 hrs favourable		(£0.25 per hr) adverse		(£250) adverse

The variance analysis would show these figures:

- Labour efficiency variance is costed at the budgeted rate per hour:

  320 hrs favourable × £3 per hr = £960 favourable

- Labour rate variance is costed for the hours actually worked:

  (25p per hr) adverse × 4840 hrs = (£1210) adverse

This reveals a big gain in efficiency that came close to completely offsetting the adverse rate variance. Surely managers would want to know how it was achieved: can the trick be repeated or turned into a new norm without the risk of any damaging side-effects in reducing morale, poorer quality workmanship etc?

The adverse rate variance might be a worrying factor – although it may not be under the control of the managers of the department. Possibly it might be the result of a wage award that wasn't allowed for in the standard rate. On the other hand it might be in part due to allowances that the managers do have the freedom to offer, or to decisions about overtime working that are within their authority to make. Perhaps they are empowered to employ workers with a higher level of skill and at a higher pay rate if they believe they can get an overall saving as a result. If that was the explanation of the joint variances here, the economy attempt would have to be reckoned a failure – but only just, and perhaps worth persisting with. With experience, it might be made to produce a good pay-off.

Overhead cost variances

Just like the material and the labour cost variances, there are the same two elements in overhead expenditures – volume and price. But it's often not worth going to all the trouble of trying to separate the two factors in every item of overhead cost. The detail doesn't aid control enough to make the extra accounting work worth while. It's most useful for those items whose costs do vary to some extent with the level of activity – things like maintenance and repair costs, electricity and fuel costs, consumable stores costs.

Volume variances are a particular problem with fixed overheads. The difficulty is with unit costs per product or sale made – how to calculate them when the actual level of activity is different. Think back to our original description of Moneypots Manufacturing as a money machine – the effect of Mary's pay as an overhead. Remember how at five orders a week her £30 paypacket added £6 to tne cost of each order, but at ten orders a week it added only £3 per order? This means that products that are physically identical will be costed differently where the volume of activity changes – which doesn't really make sense. Can you imagine the difficulties of the stock controller with a stock of finished goods all exactly the same, but which the accounts value at different amounts of money?

Standard costing provides a way around this problem. For instance, in the Moneypots Production budget on page 111, we've assumed these overhead costs are fixed:

Management salaries	£9 600
Depreciation	£3 000
	£12 600

Let's assume that a standard cost of £5 per unit of product has been calculated for these particular overheads. At the budgeted production of 2520 units, this figure gives a total cost exactly corresponding with the budgeted fixed overheads:

2520 units × £5 per unit = £12 600

As the accountants say, the overheads are 'recovered' exactly at this production rate.

If actual production during the period were only 2420 units, charging the standard £5 per unit to the product costs would give a total that is less than these overheads really are:

2420 units × £5 per unit = £12 100

So for these fixed overheads the accountant reports an adverse volume variance of £500. This is the amount by which the overheads have been 'under-recovered' in production. If production had been higher than budget:

2620 units × £5 per unit = £13 100

. . . the overheads would have been 'over-recovered' by £500, and the accountant would report it as a favourable volume variance.

Are these kinds of variances controllable or not? Often not. It becomes a question of whether the volumes of production or sales (which actually create the variances) are controllable – and if so, by whom. Could managers have prevented the machine breakdowns or production bottlenecks or admin hiccups or lack of orders that have caused a shortfall? Not one but several managers are likely to be involved. One important question may be how well they cooperated and tried to coordinate their different operations.

To help further in pinning down the factors that are controllable by managers at different levels, a useful analysis of overheads is to distinguish between *working efficiency* and *available capacity*: did a volume variance happen because people performed above or below expectations in a given time, or because they worked longer or shorter hours? Supervisors and other first-level managers often have little control over capacity – the hours worked by their people. But they may have quite an influence over efficiency – how much was achieved in the time.

In looking at overhead variances, an important distinction to make is between overheads that can be *calculated* in the budget, and those that have to be *decided*. Let's try and explain that.

There are many overhead costs that are either 'fixed' by some external factor or that vary with the level of activity: either way they can be calculated. Examples of costs that are variable, at least partly, are maintenance, electricity and so on. Example of externally fixed costs are things like rent and rates, insurance, depreciation charges (depending on what depreciation method you use, which we'll discuss later). As a manager, you can't arrive at a budget figure for any one of them simply by deciding you're going to spend so much on it in the next period. You're either given what it'll cost (the fixed costs) or you work it out from the level of activity the business as a whole can expect (the variable costs).

But there are other budgeted costs that do depend on decisions – for instance, the costs of training your staff. They aren't variable – that is, they don't respond to the level of activity, going up and down as your operation becomes more busy or less busy. Nor are they externally fixed like an insurance premium. *You fix them.* You decide what training should be done, and the costs are the outcome of your decisions. Many departmental costs are like this – depending on managerial judgement rather than accountancy calculations:

- training and development costs
- admin and secretarial costs
- accounting and legal costs
- selling and advertising costs
- research and development costs
- management costs

For these kinds of costs, budgetary control has a different meaning. *A favourable variance isn't necessarily a good thing.* With a calculated or externally fixed cost, if you can make some saving on the budget figure it's usually an advantage to the company: you can use the budgeted cost as a yardstick to assess the standard of economy (not the only one, but an important one). With a fixed cost that results from a management decision, a saving on budget may well be a false economy: the budgeted cost isn't a yardstick of economy, more a limit to be observed. For instance a 'saving' on training may cost you in low ability and poor job interest in the long run. A 'saving' on production planning and control may eventually run up a heavy bill in labour inefficiencies and materials usage. A 'saving' on research may become an expensive contribution to obsolescent products and outdated techniques. A 'saving' in the advertising budget may prove very damaging in lost sales. And a 'saving' in management costs may turn out to be a poor bargain in every way. We're not suggesting that once the money for things like these has been budgeted, managers should spend it regardless. It still makes sense to look for reasonable economies, but they're not quite the same source of satisfaction as a saving on calculated costs. *Rather than look for savings, look for better value for the money spent.*

Sales revenue variances

The two factors – volume and price – obviously apply just as much to revenue as they do to costs. You might be above or below budget because you sold more or fewer products than you aimed to sell, or because your price was above or below the budgeted selling price. More likely there are variances in *both* factors:

Sales revenue: variance report			
	quantity	*price*	*revenue*
Budget	2400	× £100	= £240 000
Actual	2300	× £105	= £241 500
Variances	(100) adverse	£5 favourable	£1 500 favourable

Perhaps the reduced sales volume is partly due to the increased selling price; perhaps the increased price was an attempt by the Sales Department to compensate for sluggish sales. Whichever way it happened the net outcome is good for revenue – though possibly not so good for market penetration (if we assume no shrinkage in the total market). The implications would have to be investigated by management.

There is a third factor in the sales revenue of most businesses – *the sales mix*. It's a factor for any company that has more than one product on the market: the proportion of total sales contributed by each product.

Suppose Moneypots Manufacturing brings a new product on to the market – a 'Coinjar', say. Each quarter's sales plan sets a budgeted volume and price for each of your two products. And in doing so it also defines how the two are to share the total sales between them – their 'mix'. Here is the sales budget for a quarter:

Sales budget				
	budgeted quantity	*budgeted mix*	*budgeted price*	*revenue*
Moneypots	4000	4/5	£100	£400 000
Coinjars	1000	1/5	£80	£ 80 000
Total	5000			£480 000

Against this budget, the actual results turn out like this:

Sales results				
	actual quantity	*actual mix*	*actual price*	*revenue*
Moneypots	2550	1/2	£102	£260 100
Coinjars	2550	1/2	£81	£206 550
Total	5100			£466 650

Despite the fact that the total quantity sold and the prices per product are both higher than budget, the total revenue is below budget. There's a net adverse variance of £13 350 – entirely due to the different sales mix. So what is the total adverse effect of the mix, and how far is it offset by favourable quantity and price variances? You could of course ignore the effect of combining the products like this, and simply analyse the volume and price variances for each product separately. But that wouldn't help you interpret the total result. The same salespeople are selling both products, and the required mix is an important factor in balancing their sales priorities.

To isolate the effect of each factor, you have to take the three factors in turn – in a set order. First the quantity variance, keeping the mix and prices as budgeted, as shown in the following illustration.

Sales revenue: quantity variance					
	actual quantity	budgeted mix	budgeted price		revenue
Moneypots	5100	× $\frac{4}{5}$ ×	£100 =		£408 000
Coinjars		× $\frac{1}{5}$ ×	£ 80 =		£ 81 600
					£489 600
Budget					£480 000
Quantity variance					£ 9 600 favourable

The larger total volume of sales, taken by itself, produces a £9 600 favourable variance.

Next the mix variance, using the actual quantity and mix but keeping price as budgeted. The calculation produces a combined quantity-and-mix variance, so we have to remove the effect of the quantity variance due to the mix. The next diagram illustrates this.

```
                    Sales revenue: mix variance

              actual        actual       budgeted
              quantity       mix          price          revenue
Moneypots }         { ×      ½     ×      £100    =      £255 000
Coinjars  } 5100    { ×      ½     ×      £ 80    =      £204 000

                                                        £459 000


    Budget ...............................................................  £480 000
    Quantity-and-mix variance                           (£ 21 000)
                                                        adverse

less Quantity variance                                  £  9 600
                                                        favourable

    mix variance                                        (£ 30 600)
                                                        adverse
```

Do you see how the calculation is worked out? The combined quantity-and-mix variance was £21 000 *adverse*, but the quantity variance by itself was £9 600 *favourable*. So to find the mix variance by itself we have to remove the effect of that plus-£9 600. That makes a total minus of £30 600 for mix.

Finally the price variance. The calculation now produces a total variance for quantity, mix and price. So we have to remove the effect of the combined quantity-and-mix variance (which we know from the mix variance calculation) to isolate the effect of the price changes. See the illustration below.

```
                    Sales revenue: price variance

              actual        actual       actual
              quantity       mix          price          revenue
Moneypots }         { ×      ½     ×      £102    =      £260 100
Coinjars  } 5100    { ×      ½     ×      £ 81    =      £206 550

                                                        £466 550


    Budget ...............................................................  £480 000
    net variance                                        (£ 13 350)
                                                        adverse

less Quantity-and-mix variance                          £ 21 000)
                                                        adverse

    Price variance                                      £  7 650
                                                        favourable
```

Again, the logic of the calculation may need explaining. The net variance from all three factors is £13 350 adverse (as you know already). But the combined quantity-and-mix variance is greater than that – it's actually £7 650 *more* adverse. So the price variance must be a *favourable* one of that figure.

The important point in all of this is probably the *profit earned by each product*, not simply the product price. So it may be useful to rework the figures but with gross profit in place of prices, as in the following illustration.

Sales budget and results: profit variances				
Budgeted:	quantity	mix	gross profit per unit	gross profit
Moneypots	4000	4/5	£45	£180 000
Coinjars	1000	1/5	£25	£ 25 000
				£205 000
Actual:	quantity	mix	gross profit per unit	gross profit
Moneypots	2550	1/2	£42	£107 100
Coinjars	2550	1/2	£30	£ 76 500
				£183 600
Profit variance				(£21 400) adverse

This kind of calculation would be able to take into account the way that changes in the volume of production of each product altered its profitability – the effect of fixed overheads that we've talked about earlier. In this case, even at the slightly higher prices your unit profit is reduced on the smaller sales of Moneypots, through the same fixed overhead costs being spread over fewer sales. There's an increase in Coinjars' profitability on the same reasoning – more sales to share the same fixed costs. But the net result is still an uncomfortably big adverse variance of £21 400 less profit.

The variances we've discussed certainly don't exhaust the range of financial information that is potentially useful for management control. Anything worth planning must also be worth checking on to see how performance compares with the plan.

Your budget plan included projected balance sheets as well as revenue and cost intentions, so your reports could also include comparisons between budgeted and actual balance sheet figures: what variances exist on stock levels, for instance? How do your debtors figures compare with those you budgeted for? What about creditors? How has the cash in the bank actually moved? You'll need information on all these things at regular intervals – and at fairly frequent intervals for cash movements – if you want to be in a position to catch problems early in any of them.

Charting the data

We've shown some very simple examples of variance reports for different items. But the reports that managers and supervisors receive from period to period have to gather all this data together in an easy-to-read format. That means it has to be presented in a table or chart so that the reader can quickly spot significant figures:

- the '*controllable*' and '*non-controllable*' costs – distinguishing those he can influence from those he can't.
- the *significance* of the variances, as indicated by their relative sizes. Quoting them as a percentage up or down from the budgeted figure is a way to do this.
- the *long-term trends*. The system will provide reports at monthly (or even shorter) intervals to connect up with the monthly cash flow forecasts and other short-stage figures that have been planned. But managers have also to keep an eye on the longer-term picture: how does performance compare with budget for the year so far?

On page 150 is a format that would answer these points. It's a form of monthly report used in Moneypots Manufacturing. This is how it might be laid out for the Moulding Section in the Production Department, a report to the supervisor responsible for that section.

Across the top you see the way the figures are reported both for the month just ended and for the whole of the year to date: the budget, the actual figures, the variances in money and percentage terms. Down the left-hand side are the various budget items, starting with the output quantity – a basic figure to establish for variable budgeting, which we assume is being used. In each of the variable cost items that follow, the 'budget' figure is adjusted to the actual output quoted at the top.

You'll notice the cost items are divided into 'controllable' and 'non-controllable' items. Variance figures are given for the controllable items only (remember, adverse variances in brackets, favourable without brackets). There's no point in analysing variances that the manager in charge can't do anything about. You might well feel the excessive plant maintenance figures, for instance, are controllable – by purchasing some new plant. But that's not a decision for the Moulding Supervisor. He's stuck with the plant he's got until a manager somewhere upstairs decides on a capital expenditure programme (it would be a 'controllable' item in the reports to that manager).

MONEYPOTS MANUFACTURING LIMITED
Monthly budgetary control report

Department: PRODUCTION   *Month*: JULY 1990
Section: MOULDING
Supervisor: A. BROWN

	This month				Year to date			
	Budget	Actual	*Variance*		Budget	Actual	*Variance*	
OUTPUT	qty.	qty	qty	%	qty.	qty.	qty.	%
product units	700	735	+35	+5.0	5200	5356	+156	+3.0
COSTS	budgeted for 735 units				budgeted for 5356 units			
	£	£	£	%	£	£	£	%
Controllable:								
materials	11025	10727	298	2.7	80340	77930	2410	3.0
direct labour	4410	4578	(168)	(3.8)	32136	32297	(161)	(0.5)
indirect labour	2205	2436	(231)	(10.5)	16068	17161	(1093)	(6.8)
total	17640	17741	(101)	(0.6)	128544	127388	1156	0.9
Non-controllable:								
supervision	1120	1250			12650	13890		
electricity	182	176			1352	1140		
plant maintenance	450	890			3150	7050		
plant depreciation	200	200			1400	1400		
total	1950	2516			18552	23480		
TOTAL COSTS	19590	20257			147096	150868		

The problem with listing figures like this is that lists don't instantly portray what's going on. Some information doesn't get through in this form. The chart tells the supervisor how his operation performed in the month and over the year so far, but it doesn't tell him about *trends*. Perhaps one item in the budget had a favourable variance for a few months early in the year, but for the last few months there's been a persistent adverse trend. It's too small a variance so far in any one month's results to ring the alarm bells, and in the year's results to date it's hidden by the earlier favourable variances. It's often difficult to spot a trend like this from successive lists of figures.

What the manager needs is a method of *charting* so he can see what's happening month by month – a way of picturing how the results are moving from period to period. This puts him to a bit of extra trouble in drawing up the charts and updating them each month (or whatever is the frequency of the control reports he gets). To avoid being swamped in charts, he would probably restrict them to just a few budget items that are the most significant for his department's performance.

Suppose for instance that the Moulding Section Supervisor wants to keep an eye on his direct labour costs. The following illustration shows the chart he has drawn up and has maintained for the seven months of the budget year to date.

Variance chart: direct labour costs, moulding section

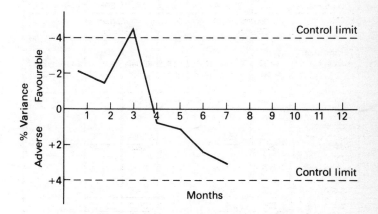

The chart uses *percentage* variances rather than the straight money or volume variances. Certainly it could use the straight figures, but there are advantages in percentages. If several charts are kept for different but related budget items, this is a way of standardising them to make them easier to compare. It's also a way of tackling the problem of *significance*: how big does a variance have to be before you can say it's 'significant' – that is, before you as a manager ought to act? Budgeting isn't an exact science. Inevitably there are going to be chance variances from period to period – ups and downs in the figures due to random and uncontrollable causes. If you try to investigate every minor deviation from budget you'll make yourself ill. At the very least you'll waste time and energy that should be spent on really important things.

Percentages make it a little easier to define the dividing line between significant and not-so-significant. On the chart you'll see two of these lines marked as *control limits* – the dotted lines at the 4% levels above and below budget, which is itself indicated by the solid line through the middle. They are limits that have been calculated or arrived at by experience for each cost element – direct labour costs in this case. They say that an adverse variance of (say) 3.8% in a month won't be regarded as significant in itself. One of 4.2% will warrant looking into.

Where the limits are set depends on the item, the size of its budget and the accuracy with which it is possible to budget for it. A 4% variance from a budgeted cost of £50 000 would be more critical than a 20% variance on a £5 000 cost. You have to consider the amount of money involved. But the percentage leeway does have to be reasonable too: because a budget item is costed at £1 000 000 doesn't automatically mean that it can be accurately controlled to three places of decimals. It'll probably be watched more carefully, but the random and uncontrollable ups and downs from budget are inevitably going to involve much bigger sums of money than the variations of smaller items.

You might be curious about why a control limit is given for *favourable* variances. Surely there's no need to worry about those? But it's logical enough if you think about it. Big favourable variances could stem from faults in the original budgeting that need to be corrected and prevented from happening again. They could spring from happy accidents that you could learn from and even make permanent. The control limits alert you to significant variances in either direction because *you want to know the reason why*.

The greatest value in the chart is illustrated in the line that has been drawn on it – the successive monthly variances from January to July. For the first three months they were favourable, in one month 'significantly' so. Since then the variances have all been adverse, but not enough to go beyond the control limit. The monthly reports don't give you this picture: month by month you see a variance that's too small to be 'significant', and you might well have forgotten about it by the time the next month's report arrives. The cumulative variance for the year is still only marginally adverse because the recent adverse variations are almost matched by the bigger favourable variances earlier. *Yet the persistent adverse trend over the past four months is almost certainly worth investigating*. It's only a chart that shows you this clearly. It's lost in lists of figures.

Remember the point of all the budgeting and rates calculation and variance analysis. It's not to keep the Accounts Department occupied or simply to add to the sum total of management knowledge, worthy as those causes might be. If the knowledge isn't used, it was a waste of time getting it. The point is what happens when you've got the knowledge. Its purpose is to enable you and your management colleagues to make better use of the organisation's prime resource, money, than you would otherwise.

A budget, like any other plan, is made to be implemented. You prepare a work plan to enable you to guide and control the work more effectively. Maybe events don't take quite the course you've planned, but the fact that you've thought things through helps you to cope with the unexpected. You're better placed to interpret deviations and to know what to do about them. The success of your plan isn't simply how closely you can bend actual events to make them fit the blueprint. It's as much a question of how much better the total result is than it would have been if you *hadn't* planned. The same goes for a budget – which should relate closely to the work plans anyway. How much better is the economy and the value-for-money achieved by your bit of the organisation with budgetary control than without it?

The answer to that question is up to you. If you've got the opportunity to take a hand in shaping the budget for your patch, don't treat it with the cynicism many managers show towards budgeting and budgetary control. Use it to get a better understanding of the costs you are responsible for. Learn how you can control them and the value to be obtained from them through your management of your operations and your people.

LEVEL OF ACTIVITY: BUDGET ASSUMPTIONS?

- FIXED BUDGET — NO ALLOWANCE FOR CHANGES
- FLEXIBLE BUDGET — SETTINGS FOR DIFFERENT LEVELS
- VARIABLE BUDGET — VARY AT A STANDARD RATE

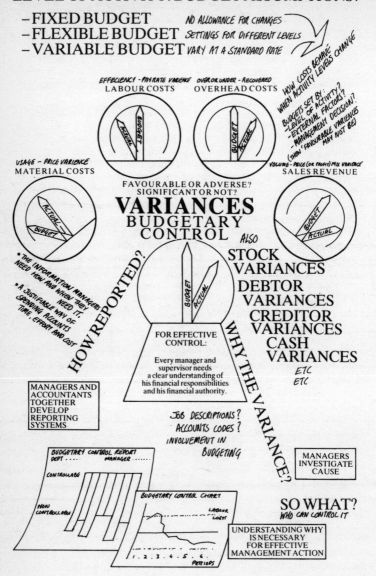

EFFICIENCY - PAY RATE VARIANCE
LABOUR COSTS

OVER OR UNDER - RECOVERED
OVERHEAD COSTS

HOW COSTS BEHAVE WHEN ACTIVITY LEVELS CHANGE

BUDGETS SET BY:
- LEVEL OF ACTIVITY?
- EXTERNAL FACTORS?
- MANAGEMENT DECISION?
  (THEN FAVOURABLE VARIANCES MAY NOT BE!)

USAGE - PRICE VARIANCE
MATERIAL COSTS

VOLUME - PRICE (OR PROFIT) MIX VARIANCE
SALES REVENUE

FAVOURABLE OR ADVERSE?
SIGNIFICANT OR NOT?

VARIANCES
BUDGETARY CONTROL

ALSO

STOCK VARIANCES
DEBTOR VARIANCES
CREDITOR VARIANCES
CASH VARIANCES
ETC
ETC

- THE INFORMATION MANAGERS NEED: HOW AND WHEN THEY NEED IT.
- A JUSTIFIABLE WAY OF SPENDING ACCOUNTS TIME, EFFORT AND COST

HOW REPORTED?

WHY THE VARIANCE?

FOR EFFECTIVE CONTROL:

Every manager and supervisor needs a clear understanding of his financial responsibilities and his financial authority.

MANAGERS AND ACCOUNTANTS TOGETHER DEVELOP REPORTING SYSTEMS

JOB DESCRIPTIONS?
ACCOUNTS CODES?
INVOLVEMENT IN BUDGETING

MANAGERS INVESTIGATE CAUSE

BUDGETARY CONTROL REPORT
DEPT ..... MANAGER ....
CONTROLLABLE
NON CONTROLLABLE

BUDGETARY CONTROL CHART
LABOUR COSTS
1. 2. 3. 4. 5. 6.
PERIODS

SO WHAT?
WHO CAN CONTROL IT

UNDERSTANDING WHY IS NECESSARY FOR EFFECTIVE MANAGEMENT ACTION

6. Measuring by money

On the face of it, money is a very straightforward way to measure business activities. The stuff counts rather easily. It's only a short step to the idea that any money question can be answered with a bit of arithmetic and a pocket calculator, as long as you know the right way to do it. But there's often no one 'right' way to calculate the money. Measuring the cost of some stock, the depreciation on a piece of equipment, the payback you'll get from an investment – they involve rather more than doing the sums correctly. Each of them can be worked out in several different ways, all perfectly valid but each producing a different answer. Without knowing the circumstances, no one can tell you which is the best way. What we *can* do is to explain what is involved so that you're better placed to make judgements about them.

For any business organisation the heart of the problem is *to know what the profit is*. Profit is a basic money measurement, defined like this:

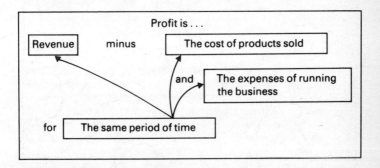

Profit is . . .

Revenue   minus   The cost of products sold

and   The expenses of running the business

for   The same period of time

Each element of the definition contains difficulties that often can't be solved simply by calculation. They require judgement to resolve them – managerial decisions, not just accountancy expertise. But what kinds of judgement? Let's take the questions one by one.

What is the revenue of the period?

In most businesses, this isn't really a problem. Revenue comes from sales, which are of two kinds – cash sales and credit sales. The amounts of money and their timing can be accurately recorded to know what comes into the period and what doesn't. A cash sale is recorded when the money is handed over, a credit sale by the date on the invoice. Count all the cash and invoices that come within the period, and you've got an accurate measure of its revenue.

But in many organisations earnings can't be quantified and timed so precisely. In a civil engineering company for instance, a contract may take a year or more to complete – far longer than the accounting periods, whether they're monthly, quarterly or even yearly in some cases. Rather than waiting until the end of the contract before declaring any revenue, the company will usually make an estimate of the revenue earned by the progress of the work in each accounting period. Obviously there's a lot of judgement involved in assessing the value of a part-completed contract and by how much it has increased over a given time-interval.

Incidentally, don't confuse these periodic revenue estimates with the stage-payments made at intervals during a contract. *A period's earnings aren't the same as the money received during it*. Stage-payments may be arranged by prior agreement and have little to do with the actual progress of the contract in the particular periods when they're paid.

What are the costs of the period?

Measurement is straightforward enough for **direct costs** – in principle, anyway. What difficulties arise are more likely to be with the figures you're using, not with the way the measurement is done. As long as there are accurate records of what goods were sold and what was paid for them (or paid for the materials and labour that went into them), there's no judgement involved in deciding which costs do come into the period and which don't.

The problem centres on **overheads**. First, it isn't always obvious whether an overhead is really an expense of the period or whether it should be classed as capital expenditure on a fixed asset. In the one case it's a cost in the period's P-and-L, reducing in one lump the profit for that period. In the other it goes into the balance sheet and then enters successive P-and-Ls as smaller dollops of depreciation. The difference in the effects on profit aren't hard to see.

Secondly, there's judgement in deciding how to depreciate. When you've got a fixed asset, how do you spread its costs over the successive periods during its life? There's more than one way of doing it. Each one will have a different effect on the costs of each period – and so on that period's profit.

Expense or fixed asset?

Suppose you are installing some new plant in the factory. To do this you have to remove old plant, demolish some walls, extend the building to make room for the new equipment and then fit the new plant in place. Your own labour will do all this work. The plant will cost something to buy in payment to its supplier. Its installation will also cost something in the company's wage bill.

There's no question that the payment for the plant is capital expenditure – it doesn't touch the P-and-L as an expense of the period but goes straight into the balance sheet as a fixed asset. What about the wages spent on its installation? Do you leave them in the P-and-L as an expense of the period, or transfer them to the balance sheet as part of the cost of your new fixed asset? What about other overhead items that also contain costs due to the installation work? Do you include them? And if so, how much of each of them do you 'capitalise' (i.e. treat as capital expenditure instead of period expenses)? It may be quite difficult to decide the amount of money involved.

There's the same kind of problem when a manufacturer moves some existing production machines from one location to another. Are the transport charges capital expenditure or P-and-L expense? Or when an airline creates a new livery for its aircraft at huge expense and repaints them all in the new style. Capital expenditure or revenue expense? Or suppose a company refurbishes a dilapidated property it owns. Repairing a broken window or replacing a few tiles on the roof would almost certainly be called maintenance and appear as an expense in the period's P-and-L. But complete refurbishment? You could consider this an improvement and capitalise the cost of the work. Equally you could claim the work was due to a backlog of maintenance not done in the past and call it an expense. You could even split the cost, capitalise some of it and leave the rest as expense.

However a business deals with questions like these, they're obviously not matters of accountancy calculation but of managerial judgement too. There are no rules for dealing with them, although there are some generally agreed guidelines on where it is reasonable to capitalise some spending on an asset:

- if its life has been extended.
- if its earning capacity has been increased.
- if its operating costs have been reduced.
- if it has been improved in any other way beyond its original condition when first bought.

These guides might be helpful if the assets are tangible things. But what if they aren't? There's a problem we've already looked at – the costs of developing a new product, of an advertising campaign that will benefit sales in periods after it's been paid for, of a training programme whose main effects will be felt months or even years later. It's possible to argue that they're all examples of capital not current expenditure. Yet the assets they provide aren't like machines or buildings – physical things whose working life can be extended or earning capacity increased . . . They're intangibles.

The real question is: *'does this spending benefit future periods so much that it ought to be charged against their profits?'*

Even when you've decided some expenditure should be capitalised, that's not the end of the problem. You've still got to decide *how much* of the spending to treat this way – and then *how* to depreciate it through the following periods' P-and-Ls.

How to depreciate?

So. You have some fixed assets in the company's balance sheet, whether they're buildings or plant or vehicles – or a product development project or an advertising campaign or whatever. What are the judgements you have to make about their depreciation? Basically you've got one fact and three questions to decide for each fixed asset. The fact is what it cost you. The questions are:
- how long will its life be in the business?
- what will its scrap or resale value (if any) be at the end of that time? This gives you the total depreciation you have to recover.
- what method will you use to divide the total depreciation between accounting periods during its life?

The life you assume for the asset depends on several factors you have to make estimates about. The crucial ones are probably: the rate of wear-and-tear; the rate at which the asset will grow obsolete; the rate at which the job it does or the things it produces become obsolete. The problem is obviously difficult with an asset of a new type where there's no precedent to fall back on. Managers and accountants will together try hard to make a good estimate of its working life. But with assets that are regarded as similar to others the company already owns and whose life has already been estimated, accountants will see no problem at all. They'll write off the new assets over the same period as the old. There may well be a problem here: are the new assets really similar enough to the old to make the same assumptions about the extent of their working life? Unless managers consider this question, it's not likely to get asked.

The resale value of an asset at the end of its life in the company is an issue only if the amount of money is likely to be significant. If so, this is another difficult decision – especially if the estimated life is a long one.

The depreciation method offers a choice between a number of alternatives. Often the choice is limited by the kind of asset that is being depreciated – some methods are simply impossible to apply to some assets. Where there's freedom to choose, the decision is quite likely to depend on the same kinds of factors that were considered in estimating the asset's life: time, wear-and-tear, and obsolescence. Unfortunately, accountants often ignore the differing effects of these factors on different assets, and use the same method for all assets, or at least for all the assets in very broad groupings. They'll apply one method to all plant and machinery, another to all office furniture, another to all vehicles, another to all buildings. But the effects of time, deterioration and obsolescence may vary widely for assets within any one of the broad accountancy groupings. It's unrealistic to apply the same depreciation method to typewriters and desks!

We'll take four of the various possible methods and illustrate them with an asset owned by Moneypots Manufacturing – a delivery van. You bought it for £15 000. You've estimated its working life will be four years, and its resale value at the end of that time £5 000. So you have to spread £10 000 of depreciation over 4 years. How can you do it?

Method 1: 'straight-line'

You take the view that the van has an equal working capacity over every year of its useful life. So you write off an equal amount of depreciation in each of the 4 years.

$$\frac{£10\,000}{4} = £2\,500 \text{ depreciation per year}$$

Straight-line depreciation	£
Cost	15 000
less Year 1 depreciation	2 500
Book value at end of year 1	12 500
less Year 2 depreciation	2 500
Book value at end of year 2	10 000
less Year 3 depreciation	2 500
Book value at end of year 3	7 500
less Year 4 depreciation	2 500
Resale value at end of year 4	5 000

Method 2: 'reducing balance'

You take the view that the van will be most efficient in its early years, so more should be charged to the P-and-Ls for its use then. As its efficiency declines year by year and repair and maintenance costs mount, less and less will be charged. You do this by reducing its net value *by the same percentage* each year. The accountants can tell you what the percentage is, given the start and end values and the number of years. In this case it's almost exactly 24%:

Look at the differences in the annual depreciation charges when your van is depreciated this way.

Reducing balance depreciation	£
Cost	15 000
less Year 1 depreciation (£15 000 × 24%)	3 600
Book value at end of year 1	11 400
less Year 2 depreciation (£11 400 × 24%)	2 736
Book value at end of year 2	8 664
less Year 3 depreciation (£8 664 × 24%)	2 079
Book value at end of year 3	6 585
less Year 4 depreciation (£6 585 × 24%)	1 580
Resale value at end of year 4	5 005*

*Adjusted slightly to round off the final value to £5 000.

Method 3: usage rate
You take the view that the depreciation should relate to the use made of the van in each year – to the miles it has travelled, let's say. This means that, besides estimating the van's life, you have to estimate the total mileage it'll do in that time. Supposing a figure of 100 000 miles, you can calculate a per-mile rate for the depreciation:

$$\frac{£10\,000}{100\,000 \text{ miles}} = \text{10p depreciation per mile}$$

There's a vital difference between this and the first two methods. They both gave a *fixed* cost. Usage rate gives a *variable* cost. Depreciation depends on the level of activity in the year for the van – presumably related to the level of activity of the business.

Assuming a different level of activity in the business for each year – and with it a varying mileage the van travels – the depreciation figures might perhaps look like this:

Usage rate depreciation	£
Cost	15 000
less Year 1 depreciation (25 500 miles × 10p)	2 550
Book value at end of year 1	12 450
less Year 2 depreciation (28 000 miles × 10p)	2 800
Book value at end of year 2	9 650
less Year 3 depreciation (20 000 miles × 10p)	2 000
Book value at end of year 3	7 650
less Year 4 depreciation (26 500 miles × 10p)	2 650
Resale value at end of year 4	5 000

We've called usage rate a method, but in fact it encompasses a variety of different methods – different ways of reckoning usage. The usage of the van could be reckoned, not by miles travelled, but by the number of hours it has run out of a total estimated hours for its life. Supposing that total is 4 000 hours, you could calculate the per-hour rate for depreciation like this:

$$\frac{£10\,000}{4\,000 \text{ hours}} = £2.50 \text{ depreciation per hour}$$

This method might be more appropriate for a factory machine or a piece of office equipment. They're both likely to be pretty static throughout their working life! Yet another possibility for the factory machine is to depreciate by the number of products it has been used to make – a production-unit method.

Method 4: current cost

You take the view that depreciation should keep in the business enough money to buy a replacement van when the present one reaches the end of its life. In other words, the point is *to protect the real value of your capital from being eroded*. The real value of your capital includes the real value of your van – its current cost of replacement. With inflation and technical improvements, the stakes go up every year.

On this view the first three methods each contain a small snag. They all retain £10 000 over the four years to add to the £5 000 resale price you reckon you'll get. That's a total of £15 000, the original or *'historic' cost*. But the replacement van won't cost £15 000 in four years' time. It could cost you £23 000, or £26 000 – let's say £25 000 for argument's sake.

So how do you calculate current cost depreciation? This is a little more complicated to explain. Each year-end, you establish the current cost of the van at that point in time. You then take the percentage of its life that has elapsed, and calculate that percentage of the current cost. You've now found the total depreciation for the van over its life so far.

What you want to know is the depreciation for the *last* year, for the sake of your annual P-and-L. (Remember the idea of the whole exercise – to find out what the period's profit is.) From the total you've just calculated, you deduct the total you calculated the year before. And there's your depreciation for the year. Or is it? Just one thing more. Somewhere along the line you've got to allow for the resale value of the van at the end of its life.

Let's work it through for your van. Suppose these are the current prices for a new van over the four years you'll keep the present one:

	£
At purchase	15 000
End of year 1	17 500
End of year 2	20 000
End of year 3	22 500
End of year 4	25 000

And that final £25 000 is the price you'll have to pay for a replacement van. You'll get £5 000 of it from the resale of your old van, but the other £20 000 has to be recovered by depreciation.

There are various ways the calculation could be done. Here is one possibility – which starts each time with the *amount to be recovered*. That's the current cost of a new van *less* the £5 000 you estimate you'll eventually get for the present van.

Current cost depreciation					
	Current cost	Amount to be recovered	Percentage of life elapsed	Cumulative depreciation	Depreciation for the year
	£	£		£	£
At purchase	15 000	10 000	—	—	—
End year 1	17 500	12 500	× 25% =	3 125	3 125
End year 2	20 000	15 000	× 50% =	7 500	4 375
					(7500–3125)
End year 3	22 500	17 000	× 75% =	13 125	5 625 (13125–7500)
End year 4	25 000	20 000	× 100% =	20 000	6 875 (20000–13125)
					20 000

Quite apart from the effect on profit, this method of calculating depreciation also affects fixed asset valuations. It means revaluing your van year by year. In your successive balance sheets, as its value increases on the right-hand side of the sheet, there must be a corresponding increase in the Capital Reserves on the left-hand side. It's what is called a *Replacement Reserve*.

The point of looking at these different methods of depreciation is to understand the potentially big variations you can get between the year-by-year depreciation costs they produce. A summary of the figures for your van follows on the next page.

Depreciation method	Year 1	Year 2	Year 3	Year 4
	£	£	£	£
Straight-line	2500	2500	2500	2500
Reducing balance	3600	2736	2079	1580
Usage rate (for instance)	2550	2800	2000	2650
Current cost	3125	4375	5625	6875

Which do you choose for a particular asset's depreciation? The answer isn't as obvious as you might suppose. Ask your accountant!

What are the costs of the products?

The first problem here is how to separate the costs of the *products* (goods or services) from the expenses of *running the business*. If you're a trader – simply buying and selling goods – it's a question of the cost of goods *sold*. Over and above whatever you pay to your supplier, where do you put the expenses of the purchasing operation, of transporting the goods, of running the stores you keep them in and so on? Are they expenses of the business, or actually part of the cost of the goods you sell?

If you're a manufacturer the problem becomes a bit more complicated. You've got to decide how you calculate the cost of goods *made* – the goods you have, for instance, in your finished goods stock at Moneypots Manufacturing. Does their cost include your fixed production overheads or doesn't it? Actually in the stock valuations we used in explaining budgeting, the production overheads were included – but is that right? After all, we didn't include the sales and admin overheads, so why treat production overheads differently? It could be argued that things like factory management salaries and factory depreciation costs are the expense of having a factory, in just the same way as the admin overheads are the expenses of having an administration and the sales overheads are the expense of having a sales force. They're all likely to continue at about their present levels for some time, whereas the number of products made will vary. So why should some be considered part of the money in the sales-packs of moneypots sitting in your store, and others be left out?

So there are further management decisions to be made in calculating the money-value of the products the factory makes. Just like depreciation, you've got several methods of doing it, each producing a different cost-per-unit-of-product – and so a different value for the finished goods stock in the balance sheets.

Suppose we're looking at the quarterly results over a year of Moneypots Manufacturing operations. These were the quantities of products actually made in each quarter:

Moneypots output	
	quantity
Quarter 1	2100
Quarter 2	2500
Quarter 3	3100
Quarter 4	2400
	10100

As each quarter finishes, you want to calculate the costs of making the goods. What are the alternatives?

Method 1: full cost
You take the view that all factory costs should be included in the cost of goods made, on the grounds that otherwise your finished goods stock will be undervalued in the balance sheets. If you'd bought the goods rather than making them yourself, your stock valuation would certainly

include all your supplier's production costs. Why should you value your own products at less?

On this basis the total cost of goods made and the cost-per-unit for the quarterly periods might look something like the table below.

Cost of goods made: FULL COST	Quarter 1	Quarter 2	Quarter 3	Quarter 4
Production quantity	2100	2500	3100	2400
Costs	£	£	£	£
Direct costs { materials used	52 500	63 500	78 000	60 450
direct labour	43 050	51 000	61 190	48 030
Production overheads	25 000	25 250	25 400	25 250
Cost of goods made	120 550	139 750	164 590	133 730
Cost-per-unit	£57.40	£55.90	£53.09	£55.72

The direct costs keep in step with the ups and downs of production quantities. Not exactly, perhaps – there are going to be variances from your standard costs – but nearly so. Overheads vary far less. The effect is to make the cost-per-unit jump about from period to period. It's high when production is low (fewer products to spread the overheads among), and low when production is high. On this reckoning a sales-pack of moneypots costs you £57.40 to make in quarter one, but only £53.09 to make in quarter three. It's a question of how many products there are to 'absorb' the more-or-less static overheads. For this reason, another name for the method is *ABSORPTION COSTING*.

This costing method creates a fairly obvious problem in valuing your finished goods stock. Identical products made in different periods will be costed differently.

Method 2: direct cost
You take the view that the point of the exercise is to find out what it actually costs to make a given extra quantity of moneypots. Obviously, it doesn't add anything to your fixed costs – they stay more or less the same whether you take on

extra business or you don't. The extra costs (what the accountants call the 'incremental' costs) will be those of the materials and labour that are put into the pots. So you cost exactly the same products as before, as in the table below.

Cost of goods made: DIRECT COST	Quarter 1	Quarter 2	Quarter 3	Quarter 4
Production quantity	2100	2500	3100	2400
Costs	£	£	£	£
Direct costs { materials used	52 500	63 500	78 000	60 450
direct labour	43 050	51 000	61 190	48 030
Cost of goods made	95 550	114 500	139 190	108 480
Cost-per-unit	£45.50	£45.80	£44.90	£45.20

The changes between the quarterly costs-per-unit are now quite small. In fact they are *only* the variances between your standard costs (£45 in total) and the actual costs each quarter. But using this method, your balance sheets would show your finished goods stock at a far lower valuation.

Actually it isn't quite accurate to limit this method to direct costs, because some indirect costs can also be counted. The real point is the *variable* costs, whether they're direct (which most of them presumably will be) or overheads. So any elements of overheads that vary in step with the volume of business should also be included along with the true direct costs. The aim is to establish the extra '*margin*' of cost for each single extra unit produced or sold. For this reason, the method is usually called *MARGINAL COSTING*.

Method 3: Standard cost
You want to avoid a fluctuating cost-per-unit from period to period, but also feel that production overheads must somehow be included in the cost of goods. You do this by ignoring the actual costs in valuing your finished goods in stock. They'll be entered in the balance sheet at a standard cost.

You calculate a *predetermined rate* for charging each

unit of production with its share of fixed production costs – a standard rate based on the budgeted volume of production. It's the same basic idea as the standard costings for materials and direct labour, except that here the standard is an artificial one. For materials and labour, whatever the actual production volume, you'd expect the actual costs to be pretty well in line with standard. For overheads, if actual production is much above budget, the standard cost will produce a much bigger figure than the actual cost. If production is below budget, standard cost will produce a smaller figure than the actual cost. You'll accept this as a volume variance on your overheads – the extent to which they've been under or over-recovered by this costing method.

In Moneypots Manufacturing, suppose you budgeted your production volume for a year at 10 000 sales-packs of moneypots, and your production overheads at £100 000. You calculate a standard overhead cost of £10 per unit of product. You have also costed your standard direct costs per unit at £25 for material and £20 for direct labour. On the actual production volumes and costs, the following table shows your figures.

Cost of goods made: STANDARD COST	Quarter 1	Quarter 2	Quarter 3	Quarter 4
Production quantity	2100	2500	3100	2400
Standard costings				
materials	52 500	62 500	77 500	60 000
direct labour	42 000	50 000	62 000	48 000
overheads	21 000	25 000	31 000	24 000
Cost of goods made	115 500	137 500	170 500	132 000
Cost-per-unit	£55.00	£55.00	£55.00	£55.00
Actual costs				
materials	52 500	63 500	78 000	60 450
variances	—	(1 000)	(500)	(450)
direct labour	43 050	51 000	61 190	48 030
variances	(1 050)	(1 000)	810	(30)
overheads	25 000	25 250	25 400	25 250
variances	(4 000)	(250)	5 600	(1 250)

Remember, variances in brackets are adverse, variances without brackets are favourable. In the case of the overheads, brackets mean the standard per-unit cost has *under-recovered* the actual costs. No brackets means it has *over-recovered* the actual costs by that amount. You'll notice how much bigger the swings in overhead variances are than the swings in the materials and labour variances – simply because of the changes in production volumes from quarter to quarter.

Method 4: current cost
In your view, your costings should take account of the fact that prices are continually changing – mostly upwards. Just as with current cost depreciation, you want to allow for inflation pushing up the costs of replacing the stock you use. Materials cost more and more, labour and staff pay rates increase, overheads escalate. How do you compensate for these changes? In principle it's the same problem as the escalating cost of replacing your van – but happening every time you make and sell another product rather than at intervals of years.

Let's illustrate the problem with your materials purchases. Month by month you're buying quantities of paint, let's say. Each month the price per tin increases, from £3.00 in September to £3.10 in October to £3.15 in November. These particular tins stay in stock until December (Production is using other paint you already have in stock), and then some are issued to the factory. The following table shows how they appear in the material stock accounts.

Material stocks: paint purchases and issues							
	price per tin	purchases tins	£	issues tins	£	balance in stock tins	£
September	£3.00	800	2400	—	—	800	2400
October	£3.10	300	930	—	—	1100	3330
November	£3.15	400	1260	—	—	1500	4590
December		—	—	600	?	900	?

What do you charge to Production costs for the 600 tins issued to them? What's the value of the 900 left? You've got several different ways of calculating the amounts, most of them based on the *historic costs* of your purchases.

First-In-First-Out. This is often referred to as the 'FIFO' method. You cost the tins issued as though they were from those you bought in September. The balance in stock is assumed to be the cost of the September purchases plus all the October and November purchases. So the figures are calculated as shown below:

December paint issues and balance in stock (FIFO)			
issues		balance in stock	
600 tins at £3.00 = £1800		200 tins at £3.00 = £600	
		300 tins at £3.10 = £930	
		400 tins at £3.15 = £1260	
600 tins	£1800	900 tins	£2790

This way the tins issued to Production are costed well below the latest prices. The balance left in stock is costed closer to recent prices, but still below that level.

Last-In-First-Out. The 'LIFO' method, the reverse of FIFO. You cost the issues as though they were the last ones bought:

December paint issues and balance in stock (LIFO)			
issues		balance in stock	
200 tins at £3.10 = £620		800 tins at £3.00 = £2400	
400 tins at £3.15 = £1260		100 tins at £3.10 = £310	
600 tins	£1880	900 tins	£2710

This way the tins issued to Production are costed much closer to the latest price, which is probably more realistic. The trouble is that the balance left in stock is now seriously under-valued at very old price levels.

Average cost. You cost each tin at the average for your total stock. You know from the materials stock account that the 1500 tins you've got in stock by the end of November cost £4590. So you calculate an average cost per tin:

$$\frac{£4590}{1500 \text{ tins}} = £3.06 \text{ per tin}$$

Now your costings are calculated on that figure:

December paint issues and balance in stock (Average cost)	
issues	balance in stock
600 tins at £3.06 = £1836	900 tins at £3.06 = £2754

Each of the three methods goes some way towards recognising the problem of changing price levels. But none of them takes full account of the current price of paint, because in one way or another they're all based on historic costs. To resolve the problem you have to use Current Cost Accounting.

Current cost. To replace the 600 tins issued, your supplier's price per tin in December is £3.20. You calculate the historic cost by one of the methods we've just explained, but alongside that you calculate the current replacement cost at £3.20 a tin. This is the figure you'll charge to Production materials costs. It will include an extra amount over and above the historic cost – but an extra that has nothing to do with profit margins. The business won't make anything out of it. It's called a *holding gain*. This distinguishes it quite clearly from profit in your P-and-Ls. It isn't growth. It's only compensating for the falling value of money.

Suppose you begin by calculating the values of issues and stock-holding at Average Cost. You then reckon the extra as shown below:

December paint issues (current cost)		
average cost of issues	replacement cost	holding gain
600 tins at £3.06 = £1836	600 tins at £3.20 = £1920	£84

The tins issued are charged to Production costs at the figure of £1920. Strictly speaking, if you're using current cost accounting to value your issues in the P-and-L accounts, you should also use it to value what's left in stock in the balance sheets, of course.

Current cost accounting first became a hot issue during the inflationary years of the early 1970s. Inflation has been reduced since then of course, but organisations of all kinds are very much more sensitive to its effects than in pre-1970 days. Even at a rate of only 5% a year, inflation knocks 23% off the value of money in five years, 40% off in ten years. If businesses don't allow for the falling value of money in calculating the real costs of their goods and services and the real value of the revenue they receive, their money will shrink, not grow. They are at risk of paying out as dividends money that is really part of their capital, not their profits. They may even be making profits on paper, but losses in reality. So it is as well to have a basic idea of the principles on which inflation accounting – which is another name for current cost accounting – actually works.

Let's illustrate the problem with the help of another business example. Change your business this time. You've got a shop that sells clocks. You start off with £10 000 capital available for buying your stock – 1000 clocks at £10 each. You sell them over the next four months at £15 each, a 50% markup, and use the revenue to buy another 1000 clocks. By now your supplier's price has gone up to £11 per clock, so you sell them at £16.50, still maintaining your 50% markup. After another four months, you've sold them all and go back to your supplier for *another* 1000 clocks . . .

At the end of your first year of trading, you sit down to work out the profit you've made. In addition to your purchases, the expenses of running the business amount to £10 000, so you calculate your profit in 4-monthly periods, as in the following table.

Trading Account for the year			
Period	Clock sales £	Purchase costs £	Gross Profit
January–April	1000 at £15 = 15 000	1000 at £10 = 10 000	5 000
May–August	1000 at £16.50 = 16 500	1000 at £11 = 11 000	5 500
September– December	1000 at £18 = 18 000	1000 at £12 = 12 000	6 000
	49 500	33 000	16 500

Total gross profit	£16 500
less expenses	£10 000
NET PROFIT	£ 6 500

You draw your £6 500 profit out of the business. How much cash is now left in the bank account for your next purchase of clocks? Let's see:

Cash receipts and payments			
		£	£
Receipts:	capital		10 000
	sales revenue		49 500
			59 500
Payments:	purchases	33 000	
	expenses	10 000	
	profit withdrawn	6 500	
			49 500
Cash in bank at year end			10 000

There's a snag of course. That £10 000 won't buy you another 1000 clocks because their purchase price is now £13.50 each. You can pay for only 740. You're in this fix because you've used *historic* costs throughout. Some of the profit you've drawn out isn't real profit at all.

Now replay those calculations, but instead of setting the historic purchase cost against each period's sales revenue, use *replacement* costs. The stock you sold in January–April was replaced by stock you bought in May. So, in calculating your gross profit, it's the May purchase cost per clock you have to set against the revenue you get in that first period. The following table illustrates this.

Trading Account for the year (current cost accounting)						
Period	Clock sales		£	Replacement costs	£	Gross Profit
January–April	1000 at £15	=	15 000	1000 at £11	= 11 000	4 000
May–August	1000 at £16.50	=	16 500	1000 at £12	= 12 000	4 500
September–December	1000 at £18	=	18 000	1000 at £13.50	= 13 500	4 500
			49 500		36 500	13 000

Total gross profit	£13 000
less expenses	£10 000
NET PROFIT	£ 3 000

You had originally overstated your net profit by £3 500. The real profit was less than half the figure you calculated. By using a current cost method, you've now ensured that there's enough in the bank account for the next purchase:

Cash receipts and payments		£	£
Receipts:	capital		10 000
	sales revenue		49 500
			59 500
Payments:	purchases	33 000	
	expenses	10 000	
	profit withdrawn	3 000	
			46 000
Cash in bank at year end			13 500

You can certainly buy 1 000 clocks at £13.50 each with that.

It's simple enough in principle. Applying it in practice gets very, very complicated. Most real businesses are buying and selling a lot of different items at different times, with prices changing erratically all the while. Keeping track of individual replacement costs is simply impossible to do. Even if it could be done, it would cost far too much time, effort and money. There's a simpler way.

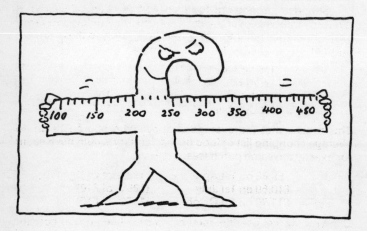

The answer is to use an INDEX. This is a list of figures, each one with a date against it. The figure says what the *average* price of things was on that date, and enables you to compare it with the average price on other dates. One of the best known is the Retail Price Index, but there are many others for particular ranges of goods, commodities, services or whatever. They are all set up in the same way:

- a 'basket' is defined of the things the particular index will deal with. For instance, a food prices index would be based on a representative 'basket' of food items the average shopper includes in the weekly shopping list. Each item is given a 'weighting' to represent how much of it the shopper buys compared with other items: you'd normally buy more bread than sugar, so the quantity of bread in the 'basket' would be greater than the quantity of sugar – it's given a heavier weighting, that is to say.
- a date is chosen as the reference point for the index. On that day all the 'basket' items are costed by price and quantity and the total cost of the 'basket' is calculated. This cost represents 100 in the index – a kind of percentage figure.
- at regular time intervals, the 'basket' is costed again to find its total cost at these points in time. Each time the cost is compared with the original cost, and an index figure is calculated to show this comparison as a percentage of 'Index 100'. If the cost has fallen, the index for that date will be below 100. If – as is more likely – it has risen, the index will be above 100.

Suppose an index of food prices has been calculated at quarterly intervals over a year. Costs on 1st January are taken as the reference point for the index, let's say, and these are the figures:

1st January	100
1st April	98
1st July	105
1st October	117

This means that the average shopper who spent £10 on an average shopping list of food on 1st January would have spent for exactly the same purchases:

£9.80 on 1st April	(98% of £10)
£10.50 on 1st July	(105% of £10)
£11.70 on 1st October	(117% of £10)

Can you always use this method to calculate current cost for any past purchases? It depends. Yes, if an index exists that's appropriate for the kinds of things bought. Assuming there is one suitable for *your* firm's purchases, let's see how you might apply it. Suppose your shop sells a wide range of clocks and watches, and it's too complicated to calculate replacement costs for each of them continually. You've discovered a Clocks and Watches Price Index, and you're going to use it to calculate your cost-of-sales for a year's trading and the value of your closing stock for the end-of-year balance sheet.

These are the index figures for the dates when your four-month accounting periods begin and end:

← Last year →	←	This year	→	←Next year→
Period 3	Period 1	Period 2	Period 3	
106	118	123	126.4	134

You start by working out your cost-of-sales for the year using the historic costs as in the following table. This is the important part of your P-and-L to correct for inflation.

Cost-of-Sales (historic costs)	
	£
Opening stock	9 600
plus Purchases	33 000
	42 600
less Closing stock	12 400
Cost-of-sales	30 200

The object of the exercise is to find out the COST-OF-SALES ADJUSTMENT to apply to these historic figures to get current costs. To do this you've got to use *averages*. You're buying stock steadily through each period, so you'll assume:

  – your opening stock was bought *on average* halfway through last year's Period 3. The index you'll estimate then to have been *112* (halfway between 106 and 118).
  – your purchases were bought *on average* halfway through the year. The index you'll reckon then to have stood at *126* (halfway between 118 and 134), the opening and closing index figures for the year).
  – your closing stock was bought *on average* halfway

through Period 3 of the year. You'll assume the index was then *130.2* (halfway between 126.4 and 134).

The point of defining these averages is that you need them to put the costs of opening and closing stocks and of purchases all on the same footing. You have to compare like with like. The common denominator will be the index figure for *purchases* (the historic purchases cost *was* then the current cost of replacing each item sold in the period, recorded at the moment of purchase). *So the opening and closing stocks have to be revalued as though they were bought when the index stood at 126 – the purchases figure*. You do this by dividing that figure by the index figures for the stock values:

- adjusted opening stock
- for the year's P-and-L:

$$£\,9600 \times \frac{126}{112} = £10\,800$$

- adjusted closing stock
- for the year's P-and-L:

$$£12\,400 \times \frac{126}{130.2} = £12\,000$$

The effect of this is to *increase* the opening stock value and *reduce* the closing stock value. Do you see why this happens? The index is constantly rising in our example, remember. You're putting these values in terms of the index figure at the mid-point of the year. For the opening stock, that's a later and higher value. For the closing stock it's an earlier and lower value.

What you can now see is the difference between opening and closing stock in terms of this standard mid-point-of-the-year price level. You can also compare it with the difference between their historic costs, as shown below.

	historic costs	adjusted values
	£	£
closing stock	12 400	12 000
less opening stock	9 600	10 800
differences	2 800	1 200

To get the cost-of-sales adjustment, subtract the second difference from the first, and there's the figure: £1 600. That's how much more the current cost of sales was than the historic cost of sales. It's a measurement of the shrinkage in your working capital due to inflation and rising prices over the year. To maintain the value of your capital, it has to be subtracted from the year's profit. You do this by reworking your cost-of-sales for the year's P-and-L using the adjusted figures for stock:

Cost-of-Sales *(current costs)*	
	£
Opening stock	10 800
plus Purchases	33 000
	43 800
less Closing stock	12 000
Cost-of-sales	31 800

This takes out of your profit the £1 600 that historic cost accounting would have included in it.

What you still don't know is the closing stock value at current costs for the year-end balance sheet. You have it for the mid-point of the year for the P-and-L. But what is it at the year-end price level? Another calculation, dammit. This one *raises* the value of the closing stock from its historic cost at the 130.2 index figure to the current cost at the 134 index figure:

– adjusted closing stock for the year-end balance sheet:

$$£12\,400 \times \frac{134}{130.2} = £12\,762$$

So you write your stock into the right-hand side of your current cost balance sheet at £12 762. The extra £362 over the historic cost of £12 400 you add to the capital reserves on the left-hand side of the sheet, and call it 'Stock Revaluation Reserve'.

Don't run away with the idea that all the mathematics makes Current Cost Accounting based on indexes a terribly sophisticated and accurate kind of money measurement. It isn't. It's actually rather a rough tool, basically because averaging is itself a rough tool. Many indexes suffer from difficulties in defining the various items and the relative quantities of each that go into the 'basket'. What may fairly represent the average purchase at one time may become unrepresentative if the average purchaser's preferences and buying habits change. In any case the average won't be true for every different organisation's purchases. What's true in general is hardly ever true in particular cases. Further inaccuracies are introduced by the method of averaging the purchase dates in order to be able to use index figures, and of interpolating estimated figures between the quoted figures of the index used.

But when all is said and done, what other option has any organisation got? If it wants to ensure that the value of its money is preserved, Current Cost Accounting (CCA for short) is an essential method.

CONTRIBUTION each product makes towards fixed overheads and the company's profit. This contribution is the money left after you've deducted from the product's selling price all the direct costs and any other variable costs attributable to the product.

Here's an illustration of the way marginal costing beats absorption costing in product and sales decisions. It concerns a company in the convenience foods industry called Snackfoods Limited. The company makes three kinds of savoury snack – Nibbles, Tasties and top-of-the-range Scrummies. It supplies them to retail shops by the case. At the point where our story begins, the company's managers are digesting the trading results they've just received for the previous year.

SNACKFOODS LIMITED

Profit and Loss Account for Last Year

	£	£
SALES		510 000
Direct costs		
materials	150 000	
labour	170 000	
Overheads		
variable	34 000	
fixed	136 000	
TOTAL COSTS		490 000
PROFIT		20 000

In this particular business, a profit margin of barely 4% is not a very happy outcome to the year. It's quite clear that some hard decisions are going to have to be taken in planning this next year's operations.

To help them make these decisions, the managers have asked the cost accountant for an analysis of product profitability. He is accustomed to absorption costing. His normal method is to apportion both variable and fixed overheads between different products as a percentage of their direct labour costs. Variable overheads of the business can be reliably costed at 20% of direct labour. For fixed overheads, he has calculated a percentage for the year's apportionments like this:

$$\frac{£136\,000 \text{ fixed overheads}}{£170\,000 \text{ direct labour}} \times \frac{100}{1} = 80\%$$

In his analysis, this is the percentage at which fixed overheads are absorbed into product costs. What the managers see is shown in the following table:

Product Profitability Last Year (Absorption costing)			
	Scrummies	Tasties	Nibbles
SALES			
Numbers of cases sold	10 000	60 000	100 000
Selling price per case	£13.00	£3.00	£2.00
SALES REVENUE	£130 000	£180 000	£200 000
COSTS PER CASE	£	£	£
Direct costs			
materials	2.00	0.50	1.00
labour	3.00	1.50	0.50
Overheads			
variable (20% of direct labour)	0.60	0.30	0.10
fixed (80% of labour)	2.40	1.20	0.40
FULL COST PER CASE	8.00	3.50	2.00
PROFIT			
Profit (loss) per case	£5.00 profit	(£0.50) loss	nil
Product profit (loss)	£50 000 profit	(£30 000) loss	nil
TRADING PROFIT		£20 000	

This seems to make it clear that losses on Tasties are the major problem – plus the fact that the largest-selling product, Nibbles, has made no profit at all. After a long discussion of this rather disturbing analysis, the managers arrive at their proposals for the coming year:

Tasties: because of competitive pressures, the price cannot be increased. Nor can direct costs be reduced. So the company will stop advertising this product and allow its sales to fall away. The estimate is that only 30 000 cases will be sold this year – half of last year's volume.

Nibbles: again, competition makes it inadvisable to raise the selling price. But increasing the volume of sales will make the product profitable, the managers believe. If sales efforts are concentrated here, an extra sale of 40 000 cases can be achieved without reducing the price – 140 000 cases in all.

Scrummies: sales of this profitable product cannot be increased at the present price level. But they can be increased if a lower level of unit profit is accepted for this year. This would give Scrummies a larger market share as a base for future years' marketing. The decision is to achieve a sale of 12 000 by reducing the selling price to £12 a case.

The managers believe these changes will improve the total profit this year. Losses on Tasties should be reduced by a half; Nibbles should make a small profit; profits on Scrummies should be about level with last year's. The cost accountant is asked to produce a profit forecast based on the proposals, assuming that variable overheads stay at 20% of direct labour costs, and that total fixed overheads remain at £136 000. He decides to delegate this fairly routine piece of calculation to his new assistant.

The assistant has experience of marginal costing methods, and prepares his forecast as follows:

Product Contributions This Year (Marginal costing)			
	Scrummies	Tasties	Nibbles
SALES			
Numbers of cases to be sold	12 000	30 000	140 000
Selling price per case	£12.00	£3.00	£2.00
SALES REVENUE EXPECTED	£144 000	£90 000	£280 000
COSTS PER CASE	£	£	£
Direct materials cost	2.00	0.50	1.00
Direct labour cost	3.00	1.50	0.50
Variable overheads (20% of direct labour)	0.60	0.30	0.10
MARGINAL COST PER CASE	£5.60	£2.30	£1.60
PROFIT			
Contribution per case	£6.40	£0.70	£0.40
Product contribution	£76 800	£21 000	£56 000
Total contribution		£153 800	
less fixed costs		£136 000	
TRADING PROFIT FORECAST		£ 17 800	

Profit will be *worse*, not better – even though the total sales revenue would be slightly bigger at £514000. The profit margin will be below 3½%. The managers are puzzled because, on the basis of the cost accountant's analysis of last year's profitability, the proposals seemed sound. But they are intrigued by this way of presenting a profitability analysis. Rather than dismiss the assistant's figures out of hand, they ask him to recast last year's absorption costed figures into marginal costing terms. He does so, as the next table shows.

Profit Contributions Last Year (Marginal costing)			
	Scrummies	*Tasties*	*Nibbles*
SALES			
Numbers of cases sold	10 000	60 000	100 000
Selling price per case	£13.00	£3.00	£2.00
SALES REVENUE	£130 000	£180 000	£200 000
MARGINAL COST PER CASE	£5.60	£2.30	£1.60
PROFIT			
Contribution per case	£7.40	£0.70	£0.40
Product contribution	£74 000	£42 000	£40 000
Total contribution		£156 000	
less fixed costs		£136 000	
TRADING PROFIT		£ 20 000	

Now the managers realise what the problem is. Labour costs – the basis for apportioning the fixed overheads – are different proportions of the total direct costs of the different products. With Tasties, the labour cost is three-quarters of the total of direct costs. This means that with absorption costing, Tasties is loaded with the lion's share of the fixed overheads. So the product is being made to look a bad bargain simply because of the costing method. The following table illustrates how the fixed overhead apportionments in the original profitability analysis had swallowed up the contributions made by Tasties – and by Nibbles too.

Product	Marginal costing: contribution	Absorption costing: fixed overheads apportionment	Net profit (loss)
	£	£	£
Scrummies	74 000	24 000	50 000
Tasties	42 000	72 000	(30 000)
Nibbles	40 000	40 000	nil

In fact Tasties made a bigger contribution towards fixed overheads and profit than Nibbles did. Profitability can best be improved by increasing the sales of the 'loss-making' product!

The managers revise their plan. They don't change the decision to reduce the price of Scrummies and so increase its sales – marginal costing shows that this will slightly improve the product's contribution. But the extra sales effort will be put into Tasties rather than Nibbles. They will maintain Nibbles at last year's level, but aim at an extra sale of 40 000 cases of Tasties – 100 000 cases in all. The profit on their revised plan, calculated by marginal costing, is illustrated in the following table.

Product Contributions This Year (Marginal costing) REVISED PLAN	Scrummies	Tasties	Nibbles
SALES			
Numbers of cases to be sold	12 000	100 000	100 000
Selling price per case	£12.00	£3.00	£2.00
SALES REVENUE EXPECTED	£144 000	£300 000	£200 000
MARGINAL COST PER CASE	£5.60	£2.30	£1.60
PROFIT			
Contribution per case	£6.40	£0.70	£0.40
Product contribution	£76 800	£70 000	£40 000
Total contribution		£186 800	
less fixed costs		£136 000	
TRADING PROFIT FORECAST		£ 50 800	

That's better! A profit of £50 800 on a total sale of £644 000 is a profit margin of nearly 8% – double the percentage for last year.

The effects of the planned changes on product contributions

Product	Last year actual results contributions:		This year original plan contributions:		changes on last year	This year revised plan contributions:		changes on last year
	unit £	total £	unit £	total £	£	unit £	total £	£
Scrummies	7.40	74 000	6.40	76 800	2 800	6.40	76 800	2 800
Tasties	0.70	42 000	0.70	21 000	(21 000)	0.70	70 000	28 000
Nibbles	0.40	40 000	0.40	56 000	16 000	0.40	40 000	—
TOTAL GAIN (LOSS)					(2 200)			30 800

Marginal costing explains why the original plan for the year reduced the profit, and the revised plan increased it so markedly. Compare the changes between the product contributions in last year's actual results and in each of the two plans for this year, as shown overleaf.

This doesn't make absorption costing useless. It still has an important role to play in valuing stock – both finished goods and work-in-progress. Eventually every product must pay its way, including taking a reasonable share in covering the fixed overheads. Marginal costing by itself might persuade you to go on and on providing goods that aren't really profitable, on the argument that they *are* covering their direct costs and making a small contribution. Absorption costing might suggest where you should look for changes in the longer term. It gets you looking more closely at the fixed costs to see whether they're justifiable. After all, given long enough, *every* cost is variable: equipment and property can be sold off, rented accommodation can be given up, insurance cover can be reduced, staff and indirect labour can be cut, managers can be made redundant by reorganisation. Marginal costing won't point up problems in these areas. Absorption costing might. You have to choose your costing method to suit the nature and the time- scale of the decision that faces you.

Investment decisions

The basic idea of investment is to get a return. There are many different ways organisations do it. Buying new plant or equipment is the obvious one, perhaps simply to replace some obsolete, clapped-out machines that are becoming expensive to operate and maintain, perhaps to introduce some technological advance that will raise output, improve quality, cut costs. But new equipment isn't the only possibility. An organisation might invest in buildings or land for its operations. It might invest in an advertising campaign or some product research and development. It might invest in a new line of business. It might invest in *other* businesses. And its investment in its own people is a vitally important place for it to put its money – into selecting them, training them, improving their morale and motivation, developing better systems of organising their work. The pay-off for all these different forms of investment might be increased sales, greater efficiency and economy, better productivity. At the end of the day it's usually down to more profits, or so the organisation hopes.

Of course, it isn't always like this. Sometimes organisations invest simply to cope with a bigger demand for whatever they're providing already – a 'more-of-the-same' kind of investment. It increases capacity, but does nothing for efficiency or productivity or quality of performance or anything like that. A shop might invest in a second cash register and another assistant. Until trade doubles, there's a negative return. Both capital productivity (of the cash registers) and labour productivity (of the assistants) are *worse* than they were before. That's often a problem with 'more-of-the-same' investments.

The problem doesn't arise with managers who have imagination and ideas about what they'd like to do to improve things. Then the different ideas they produce are competing for the money, and the investment decisions are about which ideas are likely to produce the best returns. In fact, from a money viewpoint there are just two questions to ask of any investment proposal:

1. can we afford the outlay?
2. will the return make it worthwhile?

Obviously, a lot depends on how much capital is available for investment. If your organisation can afford only some but not all of several different investment proposals put forward, you have a method of selection: you cost each proposal and evaluate its returns by one method or another; then you rank the proposals in order of preference, depending on the expected returns – the best proposal first, the next best second and so on. The list might look like the table below.

Proposal ranking	Capital required	Cumulative requirement
1	£15 000	£15 000
2	£10 000	£25 000
3	£70 000	£95 000
4	£8 000	£103 000
5	£12 000	£115 000

Only £100 000 is available. Proposals 1, 2 and 3 are accepted. Proposals 4 and 5 have to be rejected. Even though they might have produced very worthwhile returns for comparatively little outlay, they are outranked by the returns expected on the first three proposals. The organisation can't afford any more than those three.

But because an organisation *can* afford an investment doesn't mean it *should* invest. The second question is equally

important – is the return worthwhile? If a proposal can't pro-
mise a bigger return than the amount invested, the question of
whether the organisation can afford the money is academic.
The investment shouldn't be made. And even if a proposal
does produce a good return and is affordable, it still might not
be accepted if it's one of several different ways of tackling the
same problem. They're mutually exclusive – choose one and
you've automatically got to reject the others. In Moneypots
Manufacturing, say, you're considering what to replace your
old moulding machine with. There are two alternative
machines that could do the job. Either would be a good investment, but you have to decide which gives you the better
pay-off.

The big problem is to estimate the return, and in some
cases the outlay as well if it's going to be spread over a period
of time. It's a major task of managerial judgement (good
guesswork too, often enough) to reckon what the extra revenue is likely to be – and *when* the money will come in. Or if
it's a cost-cutting rather than a revenue-earning exercise, what
the savings will be on money outflows – and, again, *when* the
organisation will get the benefit of them. It's a question of how
you compare the values of the money spent and the money
earned or saved: do you or don't you consider the time-cost of
the money invested while you're waiting for the returns to
materialise? Remember the effects of interest rates and inflation! Anyway, proposals for investment inside the business
are always in competition with external investments. Perhaps
the organisation could get more for its money if it put the stuff
into loans outside the business or investment purchases or
shares in other companies.

The decision is rarely just a financial one. Often the question of what value is gained from investments can't be answered solely by money calculations. Sometimes it's simply impossible to put a cash value on them. A training programme or a management selection exercise or a system-improvement project may be of enormous value to the organisation, but it has to be undertaken as an act of faith and good judgement, based more on your understanding of the people involved and your prediction of their response than on any reckoning of financial consequences. A decision to launch into a new line of business may have a lot more to do with managerial hunch or a nose for the market than a careful calculation of costs and revenues. There are limits to what the financial arithmetic can tell you about the advisability or otherwise of putting the organisation's funds into this project or that programme.

But this isn't to say the arithmetic isn't worth doing. When you make decisions that have to operate in the misty uncertainties of months or years ahead into the future, you need any hard information you can get to guide and support your managerial experience, judgement and intuition. And if the organisation is buying long-lived assets like buildings and plant plus stocks of goods or materials or whatever, they're going to make quite a difference to its profitability for some time to come. If you and your management colleagues eventually discover you've made a bad investment, you may have to sell out expensively acquired assets at a heavy loss to recover your mistake.

So how can you calculate the money? In practice there are four basic methods. Two are fairly simple – the 'Pay-back' and 'Return on Investment' methods. The other two are fairly sophisticated – the 'Discounted Cash Flow' and 'Net Present Value' methods. Remember, whatever the method, all we're concerned with is *cash* coming into and going out of the company. You ignore depreciation in calculating the figures because it doesn't affect the cash, as we've seen already.

Let's return to Moneypots Manufacturing once more for our investment example – your moulding machine that needs replacing. It is early 1990 and you have had the old machine for several years. Compared with modern machines it is expensive in labour time and limited in capacity. It also is causing an increasing wastage of costly material, and despite careful maintenance is breaking down more and more frequently. This means expensive hold-ups in production.

As a replacement you have two alternative machines in mind. Which should you choose?

– *The Alpha Moulder* costs £20 000. Its capacity is higher

than your existing machine and it will certainly be more economical in material, labour and maintenance. On the other hand it gives you little scope to change your product design, something you are convinced will be needed within the next two or three years to maintain and increase moneypot sales. By four years hence this machine will be coming to the end of its useful life and will itself need replacement.

Converting these practical effects into financial terms, you come up with these cash savings from the Alpha during the next four years:

1991	£8 000
1992	£12 000
1993	£10 000
1994	£2 000

- *The Omega Moulder* is much more expensive at £50 000. But its capacity and economy are even better than the Alpha. Even more important, it will enable you to produce a new moneypot design in two years' time which will make it possible to increase sales and so take fuller advantage of the extra production capacity. The machine will have a productive life of at least six years.

Your research and estimates of the returns shows these cash benefits to the company during those six years:

1991	£10 000
1992	£15 000
1993	£25 000
1994	£20 000
1995	£16 000
1996	£12 000

How does each of the four methods of evaluating investments compare your two alternatives?

1. *Pay-back period*
You simply calculate how long it will take to recover the outlay on each machine, as shown on the next page.

Moulder Investment Proposals: Pay-back periods			
	Alpha Moulder cash-flows		Omega Moulder cash-flows
Outlay 1990:	(£20 000)	Outlay 1990:	(£50 000)
Gains 1991:	£8 000	Gains 1991:	£10 000
1992:	£12 000	1992:	£15 000
	£20 000	1993:	£25 000
			£50 000
PAYBACK PERIOD	2 years	PAYBACK PERIOD:	3 years

Remember that figures in brackets are cash outflows; without brackets they're inflows.

The Alpha Moulder will recover its outlay one year sooner than the Omega Moulder will. On the basis of payback you choose the Alpha.

Obviously this method has severe limitations because of the way it ignores any gains after the initial outlay has been recovered – or even whether there *are* any further gains. An investment that barely pays for itself would hardly be an attractive proposition, yet according to the pay-back method it might be quite acceptable. But the method does have its uses in some circumstances:
 – if money is short and it's particularly important to avoid risks with it. Investments with a quick return may be necessary to keep the organisation solvent.
 – if the organisation is in a quick-change business like the fashion trade, or is involved with a rapidly developing technology. To minimise the risk of being left holding useless stock in its warehouse or obsolete equiment in its factories or offices, the organisation would want investments in such assets to pay for themselves before their time runs out.
In fact, because of its simplicity this method is one that many, many managers rely on – even when neither of these conditions applies. Poor investment decisions are often the result.

2. *Return on investment*
This method does take account of the gains over the full life of the investment. You calculate the total profit – total gains minus the outlay – and divide it by the number of years the investment will run. This gives you the average annual profit. You then convert this into a percentage of the actual outlay to find out the profitability of the investment, as the following illustration shows.

Moulder Investment Proposals: Return on investment			
Alpha Moulder cash-flows		Omega Moulder cash-flows	
Outlay 1990:	(£20 000)	Outlay 1990:	(£50 000)
Gains 1991:	£8 000	Gains 1991:	£10 000
1992:	£12 000	1992:	£15 000
1993:	£10 000	1993:	£25 000
1994:	£2 000	1994:	£20 000
Total gains:	£32 000	1995:	£16 000
		1996:	£12 000
		Total gains:	£98 000
Profit: £12 000 over 4 years = £3 000 per year		Profit: £48 000 over 6 years = £8 000 per year	
ANNUAL RETURN ON INVESTMENT: $\frac{£3 000}{£20 000} \times \frac{100}{1} = 15\%$		ANNUAL RETURN ON INVESTMENT: $\frac{£8 000}{£50 000} \times \frac{100}{1} = 16\%$	

The difference is marginal, but slightly favours the Omega Moulder. On the basis of return on investment you choose the Omega.

The method does have the advantage of including all the gains from an investment over the whole of its life. The main criticism of it is that it's a rather blunt tool for investment decisions because of the way it averages out the profit over the successive years. An investment whose profits start low and then increase as time goes on may give exactly the same figure as an investment whose profits start high and then reduce. Yet the timing of the cash flows may have a big effect on their attractiveness as an investment proposition.

This method is nevertheless the most common of all for evaluating investments.

3. Discounted cash flow
Like Return on Investment, this method takes account of all the costs and gains over the life of an investment. But it also takes account of the TIMING of the cash flows. Remember that money always has *time-costs* that mount up through the period between paying the cash out and getting the cash gains back in. Discounted Cash Flow enables you to allow for these costs. The method is called DCF for short.

To explain how DCF works, let's start with something we've discussed already – compound interest. Remember? If you're doubtful, look back at Problem 3 in the number problems we set you in Chapter One. A £100 loan at an interest rate of 20% per year accumulates at an ever-increasing rate in successive years.

now:	£100
1 year later	£120
2 years later:	£144
3 years later:	£173
4 years later:	£207
5 years later:	£249
6 years later:	£299

Only six years later, the £100 has become almost three times the amount originally borrowed. In other words, compounding calculates the *future* value of a *present* sum of money.

Discounting is the opposite of compound interest. It's a way of calculating the *present* value of a *future* sum of money. Suppose, instead of asking what £100 at 20% a year would be worth in six years, we asked what £100 in six years' time would be worth *now*. The calculation has to be turned on its head:

6 years on:	£100
5 years on:	£83
4 years on:	£69
3 years on:	£58
2 years on:	£48
1 year on:	£40
now:	£33

Six years back, the £100 is worth just a third of the amount. Which is exactly what you might expect. If six years on at 20% the money value grows to three times the amount, six years back at 20% it's bound to shrink to a third. Discounting is compound interest worked backwards. It says in effect: "if these will be the amounts and timings of your payments (or reductions in earnings) and these are the amounts and timings of your receipts (or savings), then *this* is the percentage rate you will be getting".

Express this in terms of an investment you're making. You're putting in £33 now, and you estimate it will produce £100 in six years' time. That's a rate of return of 20%. If you could get your return sooner, a smaller amount would give you the same 20% – the list shows how much sooner, how much smaller. If you could get £69 in four years' time, that would be as good as £100 in six years. Discounting at 20%, they're both worth £33 in today's money.

That's the principle. Now here's the problem. You're considering an investment that would create different amounts of

DISCOUNTING FACTORS

Interest Rates

Years	1%	2%	3%	4%	5%	6%	7%	8%	9%	10%	11%	12%	13%
1	.9901	.9804	.9709	.9615	.9524	.9434	.9346	.9259	.9174	.9091	.9009	.8929	.8850
2	.9803	.9612	.9426	.9246	.9070	.8900	.8734	.8573	.8417	.8264	.8116	.7972	.7831
3	.9706	.9423	.9151	.8890	.8638	.8396	.8163	.7938	.7722	.7513	.7312	.7118	.6931
4	.9610	.9238	.8885	.8548	.8227	.7921	.7629	.7350	.7084	.6830	.6587	.6355	.6133
5	.9515	.9057	.8626	.8219	.7835	.7473	.7130	.6806	.6499	.6209	.5935	.5674	.5428
6	.9420	.8880	.8375	.7903	.7462	.7050	.6663	.6302	.5963	.5645	.5346	.5066	.4803
7	.9327	.8706	.8131	.7599	.7107	.6651	.6227	.5835	.5470	.5132	.4817	.4523	.4251
8	.9235	.8535	.7894	.7307	.6768	.6274	.5820	.5403	.5019	.4665	.4339	.4039	.3762
9	.9143	.8368	.7664	.7026	.6446	.5919	.5439	.5002	.4604	.4241	.3909	.3606	.3329
10	.9053	.8203	.7441	.6756	.6139	.5584	.5083	.4632	.4224	.3855	.3522	.3220	.2946

Interest rates

Years	14 %	15%	16%	17%	18%	19%	20%	21%	22%	23%	24%	25%
1	.8772	.8696	.8621	.8547	.8475	.8403	.8333	.8264	.8197	.8130	.8065	.8000
2	.7695	.7561	.7432	.7305	.7182	.7062	.6944	.6830	.6719	.6610	.6504	.6400
3	.6750	.6575	.6407	.6244	.6086	.5934	.5787	.5645	.5507	.5374	.5245	.5120
4	.5921	.5718	.5523	.5337	.5158	.4987	.4823	.4665	.4514	.4369	.4230	.4096
5	.5194	.4972	.4761	.4561	.4371	.4190	.4019	.3855	.3700	.3552	.3411	.3277
6	.4556	.4323	.4104	.3898	.3704	.3521	.3349	.3186	.3033	.2888	.2751	.2621
7	.3996	.3759	.3538	.3332	.3139	.2959	.2791	.2633	.2486	.2348	.2218	.2097
8	.3506	.3269	.3050	.2848	.2660	.2487	.2326	.2176	.2038	.1908	.1789	.1678
9	.3075	.2843	.2630	.2434	.2255	.2090	.1938	.1799	.1670	.1552	.1443	.1342
10	.2679	.2472	.2267	.2080	.1911	.1756	.1615	.1486	.1369	.1262	.1164	.1074

cash inflows and outflows at different times into the future. *At what percentage rate must you discount them all to find the actual rate of return in today's money*? Using DCF you can establish what that percentage is.

The way this is calculated is by using what are called DISCOUNTING FACTORS. You get these factors from a table. Across the top are the different percentages, and below each one is a list of decimal figures for successive years into the future. These decimals are the discounting factors for that particular percentage rate.

On page 197 is a table for percentage rates from 1% to 25%. It gives their discounting factors for up to 10 years forward. If it looks complicated, don't worry – it's actually quite easy to use.

Let's explain with an example – the investment you're considering is the Alpha Moulder. What you have to discover is the percentage rate at which the £20 000 you've got to pay for it now is exactly cancelled out by the gains you've estimated, *discounted at that rate*. You have to experiment a bit. Suppose you start by trying a 24% rate:

– in its first year, the investment will produce a gain of £8 000, you estimate. Find the 24% list of factors in the table, and look up the factor for year 1. It is .8065 so you multiply by that figure:

£8 000 × .8065 = £6 452

This means that £8 000 in a year's time is worth £6 452 today when it's discounted at a rate of 24%

– in its second year, you estimate the investment will produce a gain of £12 000. You look up the factor for year 2 in the 24% rate column. It is .6504 so again you multiply.

£12 000 × .6504 = £7 805

That's what £12 000 in two years' time is worth today when it's discounted at a rate of 24%. Got it? And so you go on.

– in its third year the investment should produce a gain of £10 000. The factor for year 3 is .5425:

£10 000 × .5245 = £5 245

– in its fourth and final year the investment should produce a gain of £2 000. The factor for year 4 is .4230:

£2 000 × .4230 = £846

Now add up the four discounted amounts of money you've calculated:

$$£6\,452$$
$$£7\,805$$
$$£5\,245$$
$$£846$$

$$£20\,348$$

There's a mis-match. The sum gives a result that's £348 more than the £20 000 you'd be investing today. So the 24% rate isn't quite high enough. The return on your £20 000 investment would be at a rate a bit higher than that. (If the result were below £20 000, you'd know the percentage rate you'd picked was too high.) So you try the same calculation using the 25% discounting factors.

Let's see how your alternative investments compare by DCF. The table below is the calculation for the Alpha Moulder at a 25%-per-year discounting rate:

Alpha Moulder Investment Proposal: DCF	Cash flows £	Discounting factors at 25%	Present value £
Outlay 1990:	(20 000)	1.0000	(20 000)
Gains 1991:	8 000	.8000	6 400
1992:	12 000	.6400	7 680
1993:	10 000	.5120	5 120
1994:	2 000	.4096	819
			20 019
		mis-match	+19
The DCF return is almost exactly 25%			

The mis-match of +£19 is too small to worry about. The calculation shows that in present-day money values you'll get a return of just about 25% on your £20 000 – *if* your estimates of the cash flows are correct. That's a pretty good rate. It should more than repay the time-costs of the money you're investing.

The Omega Moulder calculations are slightly more problematic. The discounting rate is almost at the mid-point between two whole-figure percentages, as the following illustration indicates.

Omega Moulder Investment Proposal: DCF					
	Cash flows £	Discounting factors at 22%	Present value £	Discounting factors at 23%	Present value £
Outlay 1990:	(50 000)	1.0000	(50 000)	1.0000	(50 000)
Gains 1991:	10 000	.8197	8 197	.8130	8 130
1992:	15 000	.6719	10 078	.6610	9 915
1993:	25 000	.5507	13 767	.5374	13 435
1994:	20 000	.4514	9 028	.4369	8.738
1995:	16 000	.3700	5 920	.3552	5 683
1996:	12 000	.3033	3 640	.2888	3 466
			50 630		49 367
		mis-match	+630	mis-match	−633

The DCF return is almost exactly 22½%

This return, although it's still a very handsome one, isn't quite so good. On the basis of DCF, you choose the Alpha Moulder.

There is a snag in this method. Particularly if an investment is a very profitable one (as both the Alpha and the Omega proposals are), it tends to slightly undervalue the longer-term gains. The reasons for this are bound up with the mathematics of discounting. As a result, the Omega proposal is put at a disadvantage. The snag is overcome in the fourth and final method.

4. *Net present value*

This method too has an abbreviated name – NPV. Like DCF it uses discounting to get the present value of future cash flows. But it doesn't give you a *percentage* figure as the return you'll get. It gives you a *cash* figure. That figure is the present money-value of the future gains *after you've allowed for the actual time-costs of the money invested*.

This means you've got to know what percentage rate to use as the time-cost of the money. Organisations get their money from a variety of sources, as we've seen already: share capital, retained profits, debentures, bank loans and overdrafts . . . Each has a different time-cost. Calculating a cost for all the money invested in the organisation is usually quite complicated. It requires the accountant's expertise to work out the figure – a rate that represents the average time-cost of all the organisation's money. But once it has been calculated, the rate can then be used throughout the organisation as a starting-point for determining the appropriate rate to apply.

For any particular investment, the basic rate may need to

be adjusted. This is because you may have to allow for *risk*. A higher rate may well be set for risky investments, and one closer to the basic rate for safer investments. Whatever the rate may be for an investment, that's the rate at which you discount its future cash flows.

You then add up the discounted outflows, add up the discounted inflows, and deduct the outflows from the inflows – just like we did in calculating both Return on Investment and DCF. In DCF we called the difference a 'mis-match', and the point was to find the discounting percentage at which the mis-match vanished. Here the mis-match is the figure you're after: that's the Present Net Value. If it's a plus figure, the investment pays off to that extent. If it's a minus figure, the investment makes a loss. The size of the figure tells you how big the profit or loss is in today's money-value.

Let's apply the method to your investment alternatives. Whichever proposal is chosen, the investment is a pretty safe one. The accountants have worked out that a discounting rate of 12% covers the cost of the money and the small amount of risk there is in the investment.

Moulder Investment Proposal: NPV		Alpha Moulder		Omega Moulder	
Cash flow timings	Discounting factors at 12%	Cash flows £	Present values £	Cash flows £	Present values £
1990	1.0000	(20 000)	(20 000)	(50 000)	(50 000)
1991	.8929	8 000	7 143	10 000	8 929
1992	.7972	12 000	9 566	15 000	11 958
1993	.7118	10 000	7 118	25 000	17 795
1994	.6355	2 000	1 271	20 000	12 710
1995	.5674			16 000	9 078
1996	.5066			12 000	6 079
			25 098		66 549
Net Present Value:			£5 098		£16 549

On the basis of NPV, the Omega Moulder offers a considerably better yield on the money invested. You therefore choose the Omega.

To be realistic, there are a couple of practical problems in using the NPV method:

1. There may be some difficulty in getting agreement on which discounting rate to apply. Even after a rate has been set and the calculations done, people may still change their minds. This may cause delays in getting a decision made. Delays can cost money.

2. 'Present value' isn't a familiar idea to most managers. But they'll be at home with the idea of a percentage return. Compare the reactions you might expect to these two opposing proposals. Which would be more likely to win the day?

- "Sir, I recommend we buy the Alpha Moulder. It gives us an expected DCF rate of return of 25% as against the Omega's rate of 22½."
- "Sir, I disagree. After discounting at the required minimum rate of return of 12%, the Omega has an expected NPV of £16 549 as against the Alpha's NPV of £5 098. I recommend we buy the Omega Moulder."

The first would almost certainly win the day, simply because it's in terms the average manager is more used to. Yet the Omega is equally certain to be a better investment financially – as well as from the operational and marketing viewpoints.

WHAT ARE THE COSTS OF THE PRODUCTS?

'COMMODITY BASKETS'
REFERENCE DATES
– 'INDEX 100'

PRICE INDEXES

methods:
1. FULL COST 'ABSORBTION COSTING'
2. DIRECT COST 'MARGINAL COSTING'
3. STANDARD COST
4. CURRENT COST 'CCA'

VALUING STOCKS
– 'FIFO'
– 'LIFO'
AVERAGE COST
CURRENT COST

WHAT IS THE REVENUE OF THE PERIOD?

CASH SALES BY PAYMENT DATE

CREDIT SALES BY INVOICE DATE

... BUT PART COMPLETED CONTRACTS?

COPING WITH RISING COSTS

Knowing what the PROFIT is:

REVENUE minus THE COST OF PRODUCTS

and THE EXPENSES RUNNING THE

for THE SAME PERIOD OF

MEASURING BY MONEY

£800 £700 £600 £500 £400 £300 £200 £100 £0

PERFORMANCE

DECISIONS

WHAT ARE THE COSTS OF THE PERIOD?

a problem of OVERHEADS:

– EXPENSE or FIXED ASSETS

– HOW TO DEPRECIATE

methods:
1. STRAIGHT LINE
2. REDUCING BALANCE
3. USAGE RATE
4. CURRENT COST

WHICH ALTERNATIVE IS MOST PROFITABLE?

RANKING PROPOSALS?

COMPARING THEM WITH SET REQUIREMENTS

INVESTMENT DECISIONS	PRODUCT DECISIONS
methods:	THE ADVANTAGE OF
1. PAY-BACK PERIOD	MARGINAL COSTING OVER ABSORBTION COSTING
HOW LONG TO RECOVER COSTS	FOR SHORT-TERM DECISIONS
2. RETURN ON INVESTMENT	
% PROFIT PER YEAR OVER LIFE	
3. DCF	
% RETURN ALLOWING FOR CASH FLOW TIMINGS	
4. NPV	
£ PROFIT ALLOWING FOR TIME-COST OF INVESTMENT	

Answers to the budget exercise

Balance sheet

The closing balance sheet (fig. 2) should look like this:

MONEYPOTS MANUFACTURING LIMITED			
Budgeted Balance Sheet for 30 June 1990			

CAPITAL	£	FIXED ASSETS	Cost or valuation £	Accumulated depreciation £	Net £
Shares	100 000	Factory property	60 000	10 000	50 000
		Factory plant	50 000	23 000	27 000
Reserves:					
capital	30 000	Office			
revenue	67 000	equipment	15 000	6 000	9 000
Capital loan:		Sales-force			
8% debentures	25 000	cars	30 000	17 000	13 000
	222 000		155 000	56 000	99 000

CURRENT LIABILITIES	£	CURRENT ASSETS	£	£
Creditors:		Material stock	35 000	
material		Work-in-progress	8 100	
suppliers	54 600	Finished goods	38 500	
plant				
suppliers	10 000			
Interest	1 000	Total stock		81 600
Tax	13 200	Debtors		121 000
Dividend	9 000	Cash at bank		8 200
	87 800			210 800

TOTAL	309 800			309 800

Ratios

The ratios in this closing balance sheet are:

Profitability (Figure 18)

$$\frac{£19\,200}{£309\,800} \times \frac{100}{1} = 6.2\%$$

This is equivalent to an annual return on assets of 24.8%. That's a hell of an improvement on last year's profitability of 10%. You hope it can be maintained through the remaining quarters in the year!

Liquidity

Current ratio (fig. 19)
£210 800 : £87 800 = 2.4 : 1

Quick assets ratio (fig. 20)
£129 200 : £87 800 = 1.5 : 1

Both down a little from the previous end-of-quarter ratios. But they were excessively safe in any case. The company could afford to let these ratios drop even further in the interests of maintaining profitability.

Cash ratio (Figure 21)

$$\frac{£8\,200}{£87\,800} \times \frac{100}{1} = 9.3\%$$

The cash ratio is very tight. Depending on the ratio promised by the *next* quarter's budgeted cash flows, perhaps the company ought to arrange with the bank a short-term overdraft facility for a month or two from June onwards? Only as a safety net of course. Barring accidents, you probably won't need it. The strength of the quick assets ratio should give you room to manoeuvre on cash flow.

Funds out of – funds into

The statement (fig. 22) should look like this:

Funds out of – funds into: 1 April–30 June 1990	
FUNDS OUT OF	£
Internal sources	
Extra revenue reserve	7 000
Extra creditors: material suppliers	4 200
plant suppliers	10 000
Extra interest	500
Extra dividend	5 000
Extra depreciation	5 000
Reduced cash	23 700
	55 400
External sources	
No extra funds from outside sources.	
FUNDS INTO	
Extra factory plant	20 000
Extra stock	11 600
Extra debtors	23 000
Reduced tax laibility	800
	55 400

The biggest movement is the money from cash into extra debtors – roughly the same amount in each case. But the extra credit from suppliers is also an important source of cash during the quarter. Hopefully the new plant will be a good economic investment. Judging by the depreciation figure, the factory has been operating with a lot of rather ancient equipment!